– Grass Soup –

Zhang Xianliang

GRASS SOUP

Translated from the Chinese by
MARTHA AVERY

Secker & Warburg
London

First published in Great Britain in 1994
by Martin Secker & Warburg Limited,
an imprint of Reed Consumer Books Limited,
Michelin House, 81 Fulham Road, London, SW3 6RB
and Auckland, Melbourne, Singapore and Toronto

Originally published in 1992 as *Fan-nao jiu shi zhi-hui*
(*Wisdom Through Adversity*) by
Xiao-shuo Jie

A CIP catalogue record for this book
is available from the British Library
ISBN 0 436 20196 8

Phototypeset by Intype, London
Printed and bound in Great Britain by
Clays Ltd, St Ives PLC

Introduction

Grass Soup was published in China in October 1992. The diary on which the book is based was written in 1960. It is unusual for such a personal record to have survived, since the terse diary entries describe life in a labour camp in western China.

Thirty million people are believed to have died of famine or famine-related diseases in China following the disastrous policies of the late 1950s. At the time the diary was written, people were starving not only in the labour camps but throughout the country.

Zhang has written this book to remind young people in China of what can happen when people submit to an authoritarian system. The political situation is now changing, but he is concerned that many have forgotten what such a system can do to its people. He is afraid of the fact that most of China's population has been raised on Communist thinking, which he defines as the idea that 'If you have more than I do, part of what you have rightfully belongs to me.' Combined with ignorant acceptance of authoritarian leaders, this is not a formula for an open, democratic China. Zhang believes that if hard times come this policy could easily reassert itself, again with disastrous consequences.

Yet he also believes that wisdom can come from extreme hardship. This is the meaning of the Buddhist saying that forms the original title of the book. China has been through hell, and is now reaching for the future. His own example shows that it is possible to keep one's humanity in the face of terrible privation. Zhang writes

with humour and irony, and his message is one of hope.
He believes in and he writes for the future.

Martha Avery

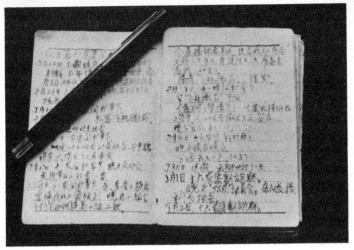

The original diary (July 1960–March 1961).

Taken just before I was sent (for the first time) to labour reform camp after being declared a rightist in 1958.

Taken just before I was sent to prison in 1970, during the One-Blow-Three-Counters Movement, after release in 1969 from my second stint in labour reform.

Note: The photographs of Zhang Xianliang were taken by government authorities in charge of the camp and the prison.

煩惱就是智慧

1960

11 July
Capital construction: hauled dirt clods.

I don't know why this was the day I began writing a diary. Nothing unusual had happened in the 'farm' where I was being reformed. I had been sent in on 18 May 1958, and had already been here over seven hundred days.

I had adjusted to it, as if I'd been raised here and spent my life here. A sharp knife had sliced through the middle of my existence – the half of which I was now conscious had been tossed into this barren wasteland. Where the other half was I had no idea; I wasn't even sure if I had ever been whole before. Hacking away at the earth, the only painful sensations I had were physical. After hurting for more than seven hundred days I was numb. I no longer felt the pain, I only felt hunger.

If this thin diary did not exist, I might begin to wonder if that part of my life was real. People have poor memories. They deal with the present – whether it is joyful or painful. But the present and mankind within it are the consequence of the past, just as the future is the result of the past. The lives of men do not pass without a trace, disappear as though they had never been lived. Many living in China today dare not admit this – they dare not face the past, and some are unwilling to face elements of the present. For this reason I have felt that I should make this most real of diaries public, also that I should annotate it so that people can understand it.

On this evening of 11 July I have opened a small diary that I bought at the camp shop. Poised to write something in it, I am astonished by the pen in my hand. It may be that I want to write this diary simply because I own a pen.

3

A pen is not a tradable commodity in a labour reform camp. Nobody wants one, even in exchange for a tiny pinch of tobacco, or the smallest piece of flatbread. In a labour camp, the exchange value of an object depends entirely on whether or not it helps you survive. Things that have nothing to do with survival are of zero value.

Except for the pen, I had already traded everything that could help me survive for a little food. And I had already eaten the food. Preserving a body that had 'life' in it in the purest physiological sense was all that mattered to me. If human beings could withstand the cold and live naked in the world, like monkeys, then I would long ago have taken off my pants and traded them for something to eat.

My pen was an imported brand. It gleamed among my few belongings. I felt, when I held it, that it gave off its own heat, a heat that was capable of warming your insides. This pen reminded me that I had once lived in a different world. Yes, that other world would come into my mind at times, but it would seem an illusion. It would bring with it an inexplicable melancholy. More importantly, the pen reminded me that skills I had learned in another world might be used in this one. When I had exhausted all other means of staying alive, I was tempted to try this pen.

The sparkling object was incongruous in a labour camp, so out of harmony with its surroundings. Yet it was the sole material connection I had with that other world. Its shimmering sparkle was a ray of hope.

I used the pen to survive. This diary was written in the interstices, the cracks of time, when I wasn't either working in the fields or writing something else. As I wrote it, the first thing I would think of was not what had happened on a particular day, nor of the thoughts I might have had that were worth setting down. Instead, I would think first of the events or thoughts that I must absolutely *not* write down. The social circumstances in which we were living at that time did not allow a person to have personal thoughts or private matters. Anything private had to be 'handed over' to the Party. This included, of course, a diary. Depending on the degree of secrecy and the degree of evasion, the leaders would evaluate one's loyalty to the Party. People who willingly handed over their most unmentionable secrets were considered to be most loyal.

In order to express absolute loyalty, infinite loyalty, some people would fabricate anti-Party and anti-socialist thoughts that they had never had. It was these people who eventually suffered most, who were thrown into the labour camps to be reformed. Among the multitude of 'thought criminals', people who were sentenced because of their thinking, many had handed over diaries to the leaders which contained a few words or sentences that were incriminating.

So, experience taught people to be hypocritical. As political movements started rolling over the country, gathering in ever more people, the experience became general, to the point that dishonesty became a common practice among all Chinese. Dishonesty not only permeated our daily lives, it affected our standard of ethics and culture – not just then but also later.

Since written words were used to expose counter-revolutionary thinking, naturally words could also be used to whitewash oneself. Experience taught people how to use all kinds of written devices to transmit to the leaders information that might be useful to themselves. This was often done in an indirect way, but was another manifestation of general falseness. And so a diary could become a work of self-promotion, written not for oneself but for others to see.

In the 1960s, many diaries of martyrs or even living heroes were made public in China. These would be filled with the lofty spirit, the progressive thinking of their authors, and they would be prescribed as required reading, 'study material', by the leaders. On the surface the author would seem to be a genuine individual, honestly setting down a record of his soul with only himself in mind. In fact, from the start he would be writing a recitation for his readers.

I did not want to become a martyr or a hero, but I also did not want to get into trouble as a result of this diary. Since I had decided to write it, it was imperative that I be prepared for the possibility that the diary might fall into someone else's hands. I had to think about how I might explain its entries, how I could safely be 'responsible' for it. Consequently, the diary could be no more than a ledger.

Later the diary was indeed confiscated, during a political movement known as the One-Blow-Three-Counters Movement. After scrutinizing it, the leaders of the state farm where I was then working failed to find any serious problems, and so the diary did not become incriminating evidence when they sentenced me. Both the diary and I were allowed to remain in existence.

Today, this ledger-like quality has made my task much harder. Li Daoyuan, of the Northern Wei dynasty,* is said to have spent many years verifying details before

*AD 386–534. (All footnotes are the translator's – M.A.)

he completed his famous *Notes on the Water Classic*. But excavating events in the memory is no easier than searching through ancient books. That period in my life is like a dream, hazy as mist – in order to make reality reappear as it was then, not only do I have to divorce myself from the present, allowing my mind to be steeped in the past, but I have to experience once again the trauma of that past.

Tormenting the mind and body in order to annotate a historical document is not something most scholarly writers experience. And yet I rejoice that I did not write this diary in more detail. If I had added just one more word in places, I would not be sitting here peacefully working today. Long ago the diary would have become part of the file of a dead man, and as such it would have been destroyed.

The notebook was confiscated in 1970, after which the inspectors began marking it up with queries. To this day I don't know why they did not cross-examine me. I indicate below where the marks were made, but the fact that they occurred in only two places shows how carefully this diary was written.

In 1980, after I had been rehabilitated, the diary was presented to me together with other documents. The other documents, performance records, self-examinations, statements by other people informing on me and accusing me, were all, as government regulations decreed, destroyed before my eyes. I begged that this diary be exempted and preserved. It has become the only connection I have now with that former world.

Can it be that that precious springtime in my life, expended in hard labour, has nothing more to show for itself than this? The yellowing pages, the fading ink of the characters lead me back, one by one, to past events. They make it impossible for me to doubt that these events did indeed make up my life. I do not want to judge the past. I also do not want to use material that has only recently become available to enhance these notes. I want the diary to stand as an original manuscript, telling people just how far the world can fall. And how, even at that debased material and spiritual level, people go on living.

To go back to that first day, 11 July 1960.

'Capital construction', which is what I have written for this date, in fact just meant building a house. We had no idea why, when we were starving, when convicts were dying in groups at a time, we should be mobilized to build a house. July is a relatively idle time in the north-west: the summer crops have been harvested and the autumn crops are already planted. In the past, farmers would use this time to recuperate. They would lay their weary bodies on the earth that sustained them, in the shade of willows, beside small brooks. Poets would look at this contentment and idealize it in verse, particularly when they themselves felt frustrated. Small farming villages have always seemed a lost paradise for Chinese.

But when the policy of turning farms into communes began, farmers no longer had a single day of ease. Since then not one of the year's three hundred and sixty-five days has been a rest day for them, let alone for convicts in labour reform camps. Hard labour is considered the only way to reform a man's thinking – like prescribed medicine, it can't be stopped for a single day.

8

The weather this July was particularly fine. People were starving, but the sun had not become any less robust because of that. She was as full and abundant as ever. I often think back to those pollutionless blue skies, those carefree fluffy clouds. We seldom see such unsullied skies today. From the 'construction site' where we were going to build this house, that is, from a raised bank of earth, you could see the paddy rice glisten below like black-green satin. A hot breeze would come in, carrying with it the fragrance of the fields, making our feeble work song a little less exhausted.

> 'Brothers, raise the earth-rammer!
> Pound it hard!
> Bastard if you don't pound hard!
> Give it to her fucking *hard*!'

Good weather and a good season could lessen the pain and hunger. This too may have been a reason I started to write the diary at this time.

Since the weather was so good, the propaganda bulletins that the leaders were issuing were especially hard to believe. 'Grain output has gone down in consecutive years as a result of natural disasters, so we are instituting a policy of "lowered-rations-to-be-substituted-with-gourds-and-greens".' No matter how outrageous, how ludicrous this seemed, nobody dared to ask the leaders for an explanation. Everyone appeared to believe the statement implicitly – what energy remained in our bodies was put into hard physical labour in order to reform.

Years later, I finally understood how the Chinese people, all together, could sink into the hell of famine for three whole years.* The real reasons for what was happening were announced to us too late, but this was not an inconvenience to us. On the contrary, it allowed us the chance to appear surprised. It gave us the opportunity to arrange our recollection of those events as though they were a tragi-comedy, a farce, rather than a disaster.

Most of the labour reform convicts had been put through 'heat treatment' in their original work-units. Like alloyed steel, they had been imbued with qualities that made them well suited for doing labour reform. Many actually felt fortunate to be in a camp and away from the heat treatment, as though coming to do labour reform was a favourable change. Just as a blind man might feel grateful to fall off a single-plank bridge and find himself in a shallow, dry ditch, the convicts felt quite relieved. Anything was better than being 'criticized and struggled against' in the heat treatment. Before, a thousand-league precipice had been yawning under their feet. Saved from that, why should they question China's leaders now?

Whatever we're given to eat we'll eat, was their attitude. Even if the labour reform camp supplied no food at all, they were there by the grace of the leaders. And so, although the labour was performed without much enthusiasm, back in the barracks there was often laughter and high spirits.

The weather was good; this work we had been assigned was also good. Building a house, strictly speak-

*The generally accepted figure for the number of people who died of famine or famine-related causes from 1960 to 1962 in China is thirty million.

ing, meant no more than mixing earth and water and gumming together earthen clods piled up into a wall. A few boards and a reed roof were then laid on top. A house was a square-shaped shelter that could keep out the wind and rain, not much more. Later the phrase 'Learn from Daqing' was promulgated, and this kind of house was given its own term in the dialect of the north-west: it was called a *gandalei*, or 'clod-pile'.

'Hauling dirt clods' is a very simple kind of labour. The earthen clods we used for bricks were not really fired – we just dug them out of the ground with shovels, let them dry and then used them. As a result, each was irregular. Instead of a brick, you could only call it a clod. Each clod weighed about seven to ten kilos. I could haul three of them at a time, at the most four. My whole body, including my belt, weighed no more than forty-four kilos, so three or four clods weighed about the same as I did. I would carry this weight, not only the clods but also my own weight, and walk with it for some fifty to one hundred metres.

The simplest things in life often cause the most trouble. This may be why leisure-loving mankind has made work into a more and more complex thing. The irregular, multi-sided clods would roll around on my back, digging into my spine at every step. When I say spine, I mean the actual bones, since there wasn't a scrap of extra flesh on my entire body. I could hear the scraping of the dry hard clods against those bones – the sound was slightly sharp, giving it a derisive tone. Sometimes a sweetness would well up in my throat, but I never actually spat blood – the only visible blood was on my back, where the thin layer of skin had been scraped away. That didn't count, since I couldn't see it. If you could manage to carry on, the skin quickly grew a protective layer of calluses. Our name for them was 'old silkworm cocoons'. And if you couldn't carry on, you had to anyway.

Hauling clods also had its easy side. This came when you walked down the road on the return. People who work at any heavy job will get a commensurate reward – for example, the road back was exactly as long as the road going. It was often hard to contain an appreciation for the fairness of the laws of nature. And what a road! It was a dry road, no water, no muck. Not only could bare feet slapping against the ground feel the warmth and dryness of the earth, they could also raise little puffs of fine dust. After I set a load down, I could enjoy the sensation of being free.

The diary starts on the 11th of July, but I must describe the work in the paddy fields that I was doing before that, or the reader will not understand my sense of release. He will not know why hauling clods was such good work.

Rice paddies are seeded in May. By July the sprouts are already at the plucking* stage. Before this, we would already have weeded them countless times. The people in Ningxia have a saying: 'Rice pull nine, starved dogs you'll find.' This forced rhyme means that the more weeds and grasses you pull out of a rice field, the better the rice plants grow – and the more rice you grow, the less likely you'll starve. Fewer starving humans means fewer corpses for dogs to feed on.

While you weed, you serve two functions: pulling up grass and at the same time stamping the field, using your feet to crush down rotted plant matter so that it goes into the earth and fertilizes it. The relationship

*Transplanting.

12

between weed-pulling and starving dogs may be far-fetched, but in order to follow this ancient bit of farm lore we had to immerse ourselves in water from May till July. The rice fields of the labour camps were created out of virgin land. When you turned irrigation water on to such land, the weeds would leap upward for sheer joy. All kinds: *sha*-grass, ice-grass, *gao*-grass, reeds, even *jiji*-grass which will normally grow only in arid regions. To convicts who had to weed these things out, all the myriad plants of the earth seemed to have gathered at our feet, other than immortal's palms, which *do* only grow on the desert.

A pair of hands were all that was required. We weeded no differently from the time our ancestors first entered the Agricultural Stage of Society thousands of years ago. We would bend our backs and pull from before sunrise to the time the moon came up. If it was a particularly bright moonlit night and it was still possible to distinguish rice shoots from weeds, then we would just keep on pulling. Sometimes, however, the convicts would be weeding a field, and when they looked back they wouldn't see any rice. A vast sheet of black water would be all that was left.

The Troop Leader would then have hard work to do – he would have to run up and down the banks of the field, looking through the weeds to see if there were any rice stalks in them. Were the convicts intentionally sabotaging production? Pulling up rice shoots along with the weeds? Usually his efforts would be in vain – the young shoots would long ago have been murdered by the healthy weeds.

After more than seven hundred days of wielding a shovel and hoe, my soles and palms had passed through the bloody stage and grown a protective layer of calluses. Legs cannot accustom themselves to constant immersion, however. Certainly not in that water. Dense with rotted vegetable matter, salts and minerals, it was more a kind of supersaturated solution. The people of Ningxia described it accurately as 'mud soup'. Every time you stamped your foot, a stinking smell would erupt from the black mud that it disturbed. Such nasty smells were insignificant, but the mud soup held substances that burned and stung your skin. After half a day, your legs would be covered with a layer of red welts. A layer is the only term I can use for it, because you couldn't possibly count the sores individually. From the waterline downward, the leg would be a dense confusion of blisters. Very descriptively, Ningxia people called these 'crazy-itching bumps'.

As soon as the bumps came out on your legs they would start to itch, and this was not a normal sort of itching. It was an itch that worked its way into the soul, an itch that drove men to madness. Some convicts would hold one leg and jump around on the other while they howled, as though they had been severely burned. If you tried to scratch the bumps with your fingernails, you would find you were 'scratching through thick boots', another descriptive phrase, used to mean that something has no effect. Scratching would not stop the itching in the slightest. The best thing might have been to rub the legs with sandpaper, but where were you going to find sandpaper in a labour camp? An alternative was to use a dry, hardened old towel, and rub like crazy.

Needless to say, legs are made of skin and flesh. They are not like metal rods – once you had scratched for a while you would scrape through the skin. At that point the itching would be replaced by pain, but this was much easier to bear. I later read a definition of the concept of itching: 'Itching can be considered a very slight form of pain.' The author of this dictionary clearly never seriously itched in his life.

The medical name for 'crazy-itching bumps' was 'rice-paddy inflammation'. Though it was a simple, common form of skin infection, there was no simple, common medicine with which to treat it. In order to make it possible for us to keep on working, pulling weeds in the rice fields, we were issued machine oil, the kind used to lubricate tractor engines. We were told to spread this on our legs as a preventative, at least as a layer of something between skin and water.

Machine oil is adhesive – it stops up the pores of the skin and becomes inconvenient when you want to sleep at night. But the worst thing was that the machine oil was not effective. In the water it was not necessarily any better and out of the water it was definitely unsatisfactory. So the question was, should one paint on machine oil or not? Should one imprison the two legs for twenty-four hours a day, or simply itch? Each course of action had its persuasive arguments. This was the sort of quandary that drove the convicts crazy.

The best solution was to get out of the water. To get out of the mud soup. We would bind a thick wad of weeds with other weeds and then toss the bundle up on to the nearby bank, and every time we did this we glimpsed that oh-so-desirable dry land. We were like sailors, out at sea for days, finally catching sight of land on the horizon. It was so close to us and yet so remote. We never knew when we would be allowed to dock, to enjoy the land's dryness.

Today, 11 July, we had finally come to shore. The diary starts this day, although I may already have worked on land for several days. Like a sailor who has finally reached his destination, it was only possible to think of writing in this new frame of mind.

The fact that I had come back to dry land was probably the main reason that I started the diary on this day.

12 July
Hauled dirt clods, picked through greens, wrote eulogy 'Shine On, Crimson Rays'.

Still hauling clods today. Hauling clods is the lowest-level job in building a house. All you need is legs, hands and the ability to walk – anyone can do it. You don't need to use your brain at all. There is no trick to it, and there is nothing like 'responsibility'. Even better, it involves walking on dry land. I could now be considered doubly blessed.

My back had turned to a bloody pulp and my bones hurt from the scraping. But that kind of hurting was hardly worth mentioning – it was no more than 'a very slight form of itching'. The convicts who laid the bricks had it no easier than we did. They didn't have to carry loads that were the same weight as their own bodies, but they did have to use a bricklayer's cleaver to try to shape our clods. When they held up a clod and tried to figure out where to begin, their hands looked as though they were handling a red-hot coal.

It would have been hard for a physicist or an engineer to make a straight, free-standing wall out of those irregular lumps. The bricklayers would often curse the convicts hauling in the clods, telling them to bring proper, complete, brick-shaped ones.

'You go get them yourselves!' the clod-hauling convicts would say, pleased at their own sense of humour. These bricklayers weren't Group Leaders, after all.* Who cared about *them*! Clod haulers cared only about transporting clods to the side of the wall. That was it. Whether or not a clod was usable was someone else's business.

---

*Group Leaders were convicts selected to be in charge of small groups of around twenty men.

Convicts doing hard labour pay strict attention to their own task. Doing their job, they become nothing more than a tool – there is no need for them to consider the requirements of the next step in the procedure. Something so simple as not blocking the next step on purpose is sufficient to qualify a man for being an up-to-the-mark, model convict.

In 'capital construction', those who wielded the brick-layers' cleavers were called 'big workers'. Convicts who transported the clods were called 'small workers'. Then there were some small workers, also convicts, who did odd jobs for the big workers, like mixing mud, hauling mud, handing up clods, etc. Each wall of the building was made of many-sided irregular clods, and all these diamond-faceted many-sided clods relied on nothing but dried mud to hold them together.

There is a joke about an irresponsible capital construc-tion worker. He tells his mates, once a house is built, 'OK! You stand here and prop up the walls, while I go get the money. Don't let go until I've got it.' The point is that these buildings are only reliably standing when you lean against them and actually hold them up. The minute you move away, the thing falls down.

In a labour camp, of course, this way of doing things was impossible. There was no money to be fetched at the end of a job, and whoever built a wall that fell down would be in worse shape than the wall. He would be accused of sabotaging production.

What was one to do? The only solution was to use plenty of mud to try to glue the thing together. 'Whether it holds or not is all in a slap of mud.' This was the big workers' secret formula for success. The most irregular bricks served the function of filling in holes in the wall.

Fortunately the soil of the loess plateau makes a kind of mud that, once dried, becomes as hard and durable as if it had been fired in a kiln. It could probably withstand a grade-five earthquake.* Of course, building this way meant that you had to use a very large amount of mud – so the small-worker assistants had to work even harder, transporting and mixing earth and water.

If these small workers relaxed for a moment they would be cursed by the big workers. The big workers were important people in the process of capital construction – they had technique, and they had responsibility. As a result, the Troop Leader favoured them, and when they cursed the small workers he would help out and curse them too.** No matter what had happened, the small worker was always at fault. Convicts who were big workers took this opportunity to use their power. If, for example, a big worker was at odds with a small worker, then the swearing at the small worker would be endless. The unfortunate underling, unable to do anything right, would have to put up with curses from the time the sun went up and work began until the sun went behind the mountains and everyone knocked off.

When a big worker started cursing, his use of language would be infinitely more vivid than when he simply made a speech to one of the groups. Not only would he want to sleep with the small worker's mother, he would also describe every part of the mother's body in exquisite detail. Both Troop Leaders and convicts were acutely appreciative of this graphic use of language; I too could

*Chinese do not use the Richter scale, they use a scale increasing from one to five.
**Troop Leaders were not convicts and were in charge of several hundred men.

21

become transfixed just listening to it. This was another benefit, an entertainment programme, that was not available when you were working in the rice paddies.

Convicts who were allowed to have a bricklayer's cleaver and work as a big worker were usually those who had been trained in physical labour on the outside. Most of the small workers had been intellectuals. They were rightists, historical counter-revolutionaries or other thought-offenders, and this kind of person could only do things that required no physical skill. When they came into the camps, they were fit only for simple hard labour. Not only in working, but also in cursing, intellectual convicts were no match for convicts who were born to work. First, they were incapable of using the language that way. Second, they did not dare talk back, especially with the Troop Leader on the side of the big workers. As a result, when you heard cursing, on the construction ground or in a rice paddy, you could be pretty sure that its object was an intellectual convict.

Don't think, however, that intellectuals let themselves be bullied all the time. There were many occasions when intellectual convicts attacked labourers in denunciation meetings. On the Outside people might not have had the slightest problem with one another, but on the Inside the conflicts were legion. This collective, this group of people, was like a mill for grinding ball-bearings. Everything thrown into it was ground against everything else. This was another one of the means of labour reform – forcing people into collisions with one another. Like a ball-bearing plant, the function of a labour camp is to process goods, to abrade them and mix them together until each unit is just like the others.

Yes, hauling dirt clods on your back is an excellent

job. As an intellectual, not only would I not be cursed at, but I could have the pleasure of seeing others cursed. I could enjoy the artistry that went into flinging invective. To hurt and be cursed too was much worse than just hurting. Although those being cursed were my own kind, intellectuals, when your stomach is empty and your back is carrying a weight nearly equal to your own, sympathy and compassion are fairly well worked out of you. You could say that they have already been metabolized. And when you are at that point, seeing others in a worse condition can turn into a kind of comfort. The perception of suffering is relative to your point of view. You need only see that others are suffering more and your own suffering will suddenly feel less.

When you grasp that point, you begin to realize that whatever can be apprehended by the senses does not, by itself, exist. It is merely a function of your own mind. One cannot then blame God, Allah or the so-called leaders of a country for disregarding the people's suffering, or for bringing endless tribulations upon a country. Nor can they be blamed for allowing some people to inflict on others what so many of those others considered to be pain. (Can't you see the carefree nature of my short diary entry on this day?)

'Picking through greens' meant helping the chief cook prepare vegetables. The labour reform camp had four Stations – a Station was a sub-camp, a division of the camp as a whole. Each Station had eight hundred to one thousand men. The kitchens for making food for so many convicts were naturally quite large. The lower each man's grain ration, the greater the expenditure of the camps on water and wild plants. It took quite a few hands to deal with all this: lighting the coal, drawing water, washing pots, picking through greens etc. The most envied job in the camps was being a temporary small worker in the kitchen. It was something like being assistant to the general manager of a large company on the Outside. Sick men, lying in the infirmary, would compete for the privilege if they could.

In a period when the rule was 'lowered-rations-to-be-substituted-with-gourds-and-greens', vegetables became the main course of the meal, not the side dish. Indeed, people kept themselves going by eating nothing but vegetables. In order not to confuse the reader, I should add that the vegetables we ate were not the kind found on a menu. They were more likely to be found in a textbook on botany. Many varieties were available, like the weeds in the rice paddies; for example, there was just about every kind of grass.

It is true that I enjoy eating all kinds of grass, but I particularly favour bitter greens and purslane. Kukucai* and dandelions are in the 'composite' family, like chrysanthemums. Dandelion greens have apparently become the rage on the tables of Europe and Japan. At that time we had no inkling of their fashionable future – we knew the plants simply as 'grass', or 'wild greens', and we ate a lot of them.

Grass that had been dug from the fields and carted into the kitchen had to go through a process of being picked through before it could go in the pot. The convicts who dug up the plants often handed over roots and all to the kitchen. They knew that they were going to eat these things, but that didn't make them more careful. Like everything else, there was a daily quota on the

*Bitter greens.

24

quantity of greens a convict had to dig up. Leaving the roots and dirt on greens would increase the weight. It was the same principle as hauling clods of earth and not caring whether or not they could be used in a wall.

'Picking through greens' was not a matter of dividing edible plants from inedible ones. There was no plant that had been dug up and brought in that we wouldn't eat. The term also did not refer to removing dead leaves and crushed stems – if you did that, you were considered unfit for the job and the cook would yell at you. No, 'picking' meant nothing more than shaking the dirt off the plants. And that was a splendid job. It was even better than hauling clods. When I did it, all I had to do was bring along a clod of earth to use as a stool. I would sit beside a great pile of grass, then slowly, slowly, I would shake the plants stalk by stalk. If a piece of bitter greens or purslane was especially juicy and lovely, naturally I would taste it. By the time the greens were picked, I would have eaten my fill.

The weather was fine and hot. The sun did its best to shine out over the land and the people on it. I would move my pile of grass and my clod over to a shadier place – I doubt if people sitting under awnings at the beach could have been any more content. A lot of the grass would already be limp and shrivelled after being dug up, carted to the kitchen and left for a while. What I ate, however, was generally buried in the middle – it was grass that still exuded the moist fragrance of the earth. What's more, after being sealed in the middle of the pile, the juicier plants would sometimes have begun a natural fermentation.

In the outside world, people used to joke about a poor man who pretended to be living in luxury. Every time

25

he finished eating, he would wipe his mouth with pork rind, so that when he went out people would think he'd just eaten meat. Here in the camps, the trick would be to see whether or not a convict's mouth was green. He would be envied and considered a lucky man if he had any chlorophyll on his lips.

The Troop Leader would often scrutinize the mouths of the convicts to see if they had stolen any greens. Clever convicts would wipe their mouths constantly as they ate on the sly, as refined and gentlemanly as though they were sitting at a formal dinner. If such a convict ran into an over-zealous Troop Leader, though, he was in trouble: the Troop Leader would crack open the suspect's mouth and study his teeth, exactly like examining the mouth of a horse. This was not, after all, a banquet hall: there was no water to rinse out your mouth! Generally, a convict examined meant a convict who was caught.

When a 'greens eater' was caught, he would be photographed. I'll describe what that meant later: if the reader carries on, he will learn some interesting things.

I, however, did not have to worry. Assigning me to be a cook's assistant, to pick through greens, was essentially the same as giving me special treatment. And so my work on this day was not at all onerous: I hauled clods in the morning and picked through greens in the afternoon, both highly desirable jobs. Only convicts who enjoyed the status of 'being looked after' could be so lucky. These were generally convicts who had 'preservation value', or convicts who had a particular use.

The former included those who had been influential on the Outside, who had a certain standing, or those with whom the leaders of the camp were friendly. For example, one cadre who was sent here to do labour reform came from a province-level post in the government. Once in the camp, he did not have to do a single day of physical work. The leaders allowed him to teach juvenile delinquents. He had a private room, he didn't need to line up with the rest of us at mealtimes, and in the evening he wasn't required to listen to reports and lessons. Then there was another man who enjoyed the reputation of being the model for a war hero in some novel. After Liberation he was Deputy Mayor in a southern city, but his luck turned when he came to the northwest – when he got to the camp, he found he had to compete with the pigs for their fodder. The camp leaders discovered this, though, and immediately assigned him to chief cook in the main kitchen. In no time at all he was fatter than any cadre.

The second kind of convict to enjoy special treatment were convicts with special expertise, some ability to do a task the camp could not do without. A driver of a heavy truck or an experienced field overseer fitted this category. These men were established as high-class convicts in the camps. It was necessary to make sure they stayed alive.

The reason for my special treatment was a temporary one. Although I could be said to have a certain influence in the world – I had been singled out by name as a rightist in the *People's Daily* – that 'influence' was completely negative. Therefore I should have been in the ranks of those who had no preservation value at all, quite unlike that cadre with a province-level position. Preservation value depended on whether or not a man's continued existence would advertise the greatness and the rightness of the policy of labour reform. Also on whether or not a man, in the future, could emerge from the camps to play some useful role in the organs of the Party and the government.

Among those of us in the creative arts who had committed crimes, however, there had never been a single model example of successful reform. On the contrary, if this kind of person were taken care of, were allowed to live, it would serve as a lesson to other writers that committing crimes was not so bad. Authors would be free to compete for the honour, thereby adding to the troubles of society.

Our leaders seem to have an instinctive suspicion of writers; they are also unconsciously jealous of them. Six years later,* this mentality was even more pronounced. By then, other than through some lucky fluke, no writer could avoid plunging to the lowest depths of misfortune.

Even at those depths, such flukes of luck could happen. I was now enjoying one. And since it was purely by chance that I was being looked after, I *appreciated* this feeling of being cared for. I benefited by thinking that I was possessed of some preservation value. From this, I developed a sense of gratitude to the leaders. This was unlike the experience of the province-level cadre who was given easy jobs the moment he entered the camps. Having always received special treatment, he was generally querulous and dissatisfied.

I ate greens openly, right out in public. I didn't even worry about letting the Troop Leader see me. To put it bluntly, inviting me to pick through greens was the same as inviting me to eat. In order not to be unworthy of the leaders' good intentions, I used the opportunity to eat

*During the Cultural Revolution.

28

like mad. I wanted to put into effect, to make reality, their kind-hearted plans for keeping me alive. My powers of digestion were substantial, and in fact wild grasses are easy to digest: no matter how much you eat, you never feel bloated. Both the leaders and I were fairly confident that I would succeed.

Why did the leaders suddenly decide to take care of me? Why, for the time being, did they place me among the ranks of those who had a preservation value? The entry in the diary makes it clear: I was in the process of writing an article called 'Shine on, Crimson Rays'. It was a sort of news bulletin, or you could call it a eulogy.

The hero of the piece was the senior leader in our labour reform camp. He was the camp's Party Secretary and was known as an Old Revolutionary. Administratively, our camp was under the jurisdiction of the Public Security apparatus. As a result, the Party Secretary was not called a secretary but rather, in the military tradition, a political commissar. When I had just arrived at the camp in 1958, this old Commissar made a deep impression on me. He was a perfect representative of our ideal, namely the class called workers-peasants-and-soldiers.

Before being sent here, I had written hundreds and hundreds of pages of self-examination. I had undergone innumerable criticism-and-struggle sessions, and had earnestly sworn that my ultimate ambition was to learn from the workers-peasants-and-soldiers so that I could remake myself, reform my worldview. Now I came face to face with a true role model. My two starving eyes must involuntarily have glowed.

The group of intellectuals I came in with had never done a bit of farmwork. That first fall harvest, in 1958, the Old Commissar personally taught us how to do it. How to hold a sickle, how to bind up rice stalks, how to load a cart. Hand to hand, man on man, he educated us in every aspect of our labour reform.

When several hundreds of thousands of *mou** of rice in our camp had been harvested but not yet moved to the threshing ground, while it was still spread out in the fields, the Old Commissar called a mobilization meeting. All the convicts from our Station gathered around the threshing floor and watched him personally demonstrate how to tie up a sheaf of rice. He used a chair to represent the sheaf. First he showed us how to lay the rope on the ground. Then he put the chair in the middle. Next he wound the rope around until he had secured the chair-sheaf. Once he had taught us how to tie the knot, he demonstrated how to fasten 'back-loops' on the whole ensemble. He said that when this was properly done, a person could sit on the ground, place his back tightly against the sheaf with the back-loops around the arms, and easily get up from the ground.

'What you all learned in school before was rubbish, useless. What I'm teaching you now is real talent! What is knowledge?' he shouted to us. 'Knowledge is the ability to make sure you get enough to eat! If you've filled your stomach with knowledge but still don't know how to grow a single kernel of grain, what kind of dog-shitting knowledge is that?!'

Nobody went to work that afternoon. We all listened with great respect to his lesson. He wasn't very tall, he had a swarthy complexion and his face was covered with wrinkles. But he had great energy. He would get excited

*A *mou* is about one-fifth of an acre.

performing in front of us – his hands and feet would be dancing as he talked and saliva would fly. His talk was extemporaneous. He had no prepared notes – when he thought of something he would just include it. The earthiest Shaanbei* swearing would roll fluently from his tongue. In addition to the regional flavour of his accent, his language was incredibly vivid. Listening to the reports and lessons of others in the evenings, for example the Troop Leader or Station Leader, we would often nod off to sleep. The minute the Old Commissar came up, we would be charged with excitement. Even being cursed by him felt like a kind of entertainment.

We were incapable of not submitting to his abuse and to his training, for he was a true educator, who used himself as an example. He was over sixty, and had a high position, yet he would go to the fields every day and pace up and down the banks between paddies, hands behind his back. His torso was fairly long, while his legs were short – at the most critical work events, his silhouette would be there, bending to the task. If he saw that some convict could not do the work, or wasn't putting enough effort into it, he would not curse the convict, he'd curse the Troop Leader.

Convicts would much rather be cursed by him than by the Troop Leader, though. When the Troop Leader yelled at people he added fists or a rope to the argument. Naturally, he didn't do it himself: he would have another convict do it for him. A convict always put more muscle into hitting another convict.

In contrast, if the Old Commissar did personally curse a convict who was doing some kind of work or other,

---

*The poorest, northern part of Shaanxi province.

he would take over the convict's sickle or shovel while he yelled, and demonstrate how to do it properly. He would have the convict stand to one side to watch, and so instead of getting hit the convict would gain a moment's rest.

'Humans are the spirit of all things. You intellectuals even more so than others! So you should listen more carefully than anyone.' He generally started his lecture to us with this soliloquy. Once, when a convict would not plead guilty and submit to punishment, would not be reformed, he spoke to us of the need for intellectuals to be obedient.

'Those who are disobedient are not intellectuals. They don't deserve to be intellectuals! Do you see that tractor over there?' he shouted vehemently. 'A tractor is a lump of steel, and a lump of steel is obedient! This morning at work, that tractor climbed up on the end of the field and then wouldn't budge. A whole group of men were there trying to fix it. It wouldn't move. I told them to step aside, and then I went up and gave it two hard kicks. As soon as the men started the motor, it took right away.

'Now humans, humans are not like a lump of steel: you can't keep people walking by kicking them all the time. They have to be obedient and walk by themselves. They can't be like lazy mules who stop when they're beaten, and move backwards when you try to get them to go forward.'

When your normal leader makes a report, his mouth is always stuffed with the Classics, the words of Marx and Lenin, Stalin and Mao. By avoiding this, and even more by not frightening us with class analysis, the Old Commissar's talks made intellectuals who had commit-

32

ted crimes feel a new freshness, a rekindled warmth. People who had been immersed in books all their lives had never run into his kind of simplicity. They had never known peasant talk unadulterated by any theory. His reasoning, derived strictly from a life of farming, made it impossible for intellectuals to refute him from a theoretical point of view. All we could do, each and every one of us, was hang our heads in shame. True, how could humans, the spirit of all things, be disobedient like a lump of steel or like some barnyard animal? We began to see that being obedient, especially to the leaders, should be a prominent characteristic of intellectuals.

During these lectures, he would often remind us of the difficult times at the pioneering start of this particular labour reform camp. He would be as casual and friendly as though we were talking about the weather. In those days, just a few years earlier, the land that the camp was now situated on was nothing but a stretch of watery wasteland, as far as the eye could see. Salt that had seeped up from underground blanketed the place in white; weeds grew taller than a man's head. When agriculturists were brought in to look it over, they simply shook their heads. They said the place wasn't worth spending time and money on to try to bring under cultivation.

But the Old Commissar obstinately stuck to this place – he liked it. He brought in a dozen demobilized cadres from the Army to look at it. They lived in tents and ate cold field rations (when he got to this point, we all started drooling). There wasn't a single piece of machinery back then – all they had were a dozen shovels, hoes and axes. Step by step, they measured out several tens of thousands of mou of wasteland with their bare feet.

They worked out where to dig the canals, where to build buildings, where there should be fields, where a vegetable plot. In the evenings, under the light of an oil lamp, they did their planning; in the daytime, with wooden stakes, they marked it all out.

Only after that stage were a tractor and a large group of convicts brought to the wasteland. To use the Old Commissar's words, it was then like 'a thousand armies and ten thousand horses gathering for the battle. The first shots were fired in the opening round of setting up the camp.' This was the one and only literary phrase he ever used, and it is possible that it was a slogan created by someone else. When he said it, though, it became his own – it resonated and meant something.

He never tried to deny that the first group of convicts, who created the camp, had died in droves. 'Back then hardship was real hardship. You'd see a man topple over while he was gnawing on a steamed bun. You'd touch him and find he was dead. Had he starved to death? No! Wasn't his mouth still full of bread? As long as you have a mouthful of something to eat, you don't die of starvation!'

So how had the man died? He didn't say.

Leaders who had some experience in the matter seldom used the enticement of good times in the future to make people work. Instead, they used the hard times of the past to drive people on. The panorama of the future was much too indistinct, whereas the pain and trauma of the past were real. They had a very concrete power of persuasion.

When we had heard these stories a few times, the tribulations of our predecessors turned into a reason for us to have to endure hardship too. Even so, knowing that the earlier convicts had been through even worse comforted us. It made us feel lucky.

According to the Old Commissar, everyone who was just starting out, including himself, got crazy-itching bumps. He said that legs would inevitably develop these blisters if they were soaked in water that was irrigating land hyper-saturated in salts.

'You guys believe in science, don't you? Well, this is called a scientific law! Getting blisters on your legs is one of the ways to reform people. If you don't get blisters, you can't be reformed!' When convicts crawled out of the water and howled on the banks from the itching, he would just watch from the edge of the canal and laugh: 'That's right! Great! This will reform you even faster!'

The exclamations that he put at the ends of sentences can't be expressed in ordinary Chinese characters. You could hear in them the kind of happy astonishment that a father has on seeing his child begin to walk. As a result, when we died from itching and then returned to life again, we felt somewhat gratified. We intellectuals had been told by the country's senior leaders long ago, 'To make yourselves into New People you must shuck off your bodies and exchange your very bones.' Peeling off a layer of skin was nothing to that.

For a short time the labour reform camps instituted a policy of not rationing grain, of 'eating to the limit'. This was in the few months when a slogan was circulated around the country that said, 'Fill your bellies: eat as much as you can! Pull out all the stops for more production!' At the end of that year, when grain became scarce and rationing was imposed again, the Old Commissar handled it differently from the other bureaucrats we knew so well. They would have waved the red-

35

headlined document sent down from Above, made an announcement to everyone, then simply instituted the rationing.

Instead, the Old Commissar asked the Troop Leaders to gather all the convicts in an emergency meeting. It was right after breakfast, which we always took to our bunks to eat. He waited until every convict was there at the threshing ground and standing at attention. Then he ordered a group of cooks to go into the convicts' barracks (these were called Numbers in the camps). They were to go from Number to Number, searching for food. After a long while, the cooks returned with all kinds of baskets containing the leftover steamed buns and rice that convicts had not finished eating. He had the cooks exhibit these things in the middle of the threshing ground. Then, with a face that was steel-grey with anger, he pointed to the baskets and shouted:

'A sin! A sin! Just look at that! We let you eat as much as you want, and you waste it! Don't you know that every grain of rice, every kernel of wheat is a farmer's drop of sweat and blood?! All that work just to be wasted by you?! Sinners! You're sinners! Starting from the next meal, every man gets put on rationing again! You kitchen workers, do you hear me? Fixed ration of rice at the next meal!'

China has an old proverb: 'The sins of heaven can be disregarded – there's nothing you can do about them anyway. It's the ones you bring on yourself that will get you in the end.' Yes, you are responsible for the crimes you commit. So whose fault is it when you again have to tighten your belt and lock up your throat? One by one, we began to blame ourselves. Then we began to blame each other. Later, when the grain ration got smaller and smaller, when large numbers of people began to die, some convicts on the brink of death were still regretting their earlier sins: if they had not wasted so much grain before, surely there would still be enough to eat today. Surely it was our own fault that we were dying of starvation.

When there wasn't enough grain, naturally you had to eat grass. Listening to the Old Commissar, it seemed that eating grass was part of China's traditional food culture. When we started eating grass, the Old Commissar instructed us:

'Eating wild plants to get through times of scarcity is one of the inherent talents of us working people! Wang Baoxun ate bitter greens for eighteen years. When Xu Pinggui finally arrived, Baoxun became his number one wife.* So what's the matter with wild plants! Back then everybody ate them to get by. They ate them until they got greedy – then they started eating fine vegetables. You all came here to be reformed, not to be landlords and capitalists! So everyone here eats grass, otherwise you won't get properly reformed!'

Before long, the convicts had no energy to work. Some simply lay down in the middle of a field. Then there were those who 'pretended to be dead dogs' and didn't even go out to the field. A counter-revolutionary theory went round about that time, to the effect that the men had no energy because they were eating nothing but grass. When he heard it, the Old Commissar refuted this idiotic idea: 'Who says that grass hasn't got any nutrition? That you can't get any energy from it? Live-

*This relates to a Tang-dynasty story and play.

stock eat grass, don't they? And don't they put out a lot more work than you do?!'

Convicts who had committed criminal offences and a small number of historical counter-revolutionaries were the only ones who had some doubts about this assertion. They continued to pass their counter-revolutionary theory around underground. Among the intellectuals, not one did not express utter belief in and servility to the Old Commissar. This was particularly true of rightists, and those among us who were zealously reforming themselves by extolling the 'Short History of the United (Bolshevik) Communist Party' and 'Dialectical Materialism'. These people had the highest respect for him. It didn't matter if his lesson was about lumps of steel or the traditional food culture of China, his was a brandnew way of thinking.

If these intellectuals, trying so hard to reform their worldview, did not follow his example, then whose were they to follow? Intellectuals who came to the camps to be reformed had long since lost the ability to think independently, for themselves. They had endured endless struggle-and-criticism sessions, study sessions, reading groups, and they had lost self-confidence. They were dispirited and weakened. With his iron-clad assurance, his crude logic that permitted no doubts, this representative of workers-peasants-and-soldiers quickly prevailed over their timidity. The brains of China's intellectuals were turned into public toilets long ago, to the point that six years later Jiang Qing could even throw her menstrual pad inside.

The lessons of the Old Commissar had a considerable amount of 'knowledge' that differed from what was written in books. But at that time one could only doubt what was in a book anyway. The capitalist class was the only one with any book education, and now we were to be re-educated by workers-peasants-and-soldiers. Knowledge turned out to have a class nature. For example, capitalist-class knowledge said analogies between man and metal were inaccurate, also that man's intestines and stomach were different from those of livestock. Knowledge of the 'class with no capital', i.e. proletariat knowledge, saw man and metal as the same type of thing, and recognized a commonality between men and livestock. Which were you to believe? You had to believe the latter. It was not a question of common sense, it was a question of class.

What's more, a lot of things that capitalist scholars said could not be done had been made reality through the guidance of the proletariat worldview. Experts said they were impossible, but the common sense of workers-peasants-and-soldiers made them happen.

Take this labour reform camp right before your eyes as an example. A few years ago, many people had thought that the land was unsuitable for establishing a large-scale state farm run by the central government. Even Soviet experts argued that this place could not be cultivated. But the Old Commissar brought in a dozen cadres and workers and they turned white salt-flats into fields. Weeds still flourished in those fields, the land was bumpy and uneven, and the whole project had cost innumerable lives, but you could not deny that the fields produced crops. From a distance it looked as though the hoary salt-flats were clothed in green.

All this was undeniable. It made you sigh and say that what you had studied in the past was not complete. There were lacunae. It made you acquiesce and agree that you simply must start again, by being re-educated by worker-peasant-soldiers like this Old Commissar.

Chinese intellectuals who have been educated in old-fashioned patriotism and nationalism have a trait that verges on fetishism. They have only to see construction projects such as factories, oil fields and farms springing up on what was originally raw land and they prostrate themselves in admiration. They see these as symbols of development, of an advancing country. They never consider the price that is paid or their effect on the natural environment.

In the evenings, when the moon was so bright it obscured the stars, on a threshing ground washed by the fragrance of grain, we convicts would sit in rows before the Old Commissar and listen to him like children listening to some uncle tell a story. He told us of things gone by. He said: 'Used to be I couldn't even read the character for "big". Up in Shaanbei when I followed Liu Zhidan into the revolution, I'd paste on the glue and he would stick up the slogans. Then he began to teach me a couple of the characters on those slogans. So I began getting a few words, slowly learning them. Now, fact is, if you intellectuals gave me a test I might not pass! Why? Tried my best to learn from revolutionaries, that's why. What I know is revolution. Lot more useful than what you're going to find in books . . .'

With great warmth of feeling, he often mentioned the famous revolutionary Liu Zhidan. 'Liu Zhidan was a good man! Never mind that he was born into a landlord's family. Little master of a landlord, he was – but when he took to revolution, he wasn't afraid to die. He'd fight on the rivers and in the mountains for us poor people. What's that say to us? It says that a person just has to try – doesn't matter what family background he has, if he works at it no one can stop him . . .' These words would stroke us like a warm, gentle breeze, and for a short time they would revive starving, exhausted, hopeless men. Although they had lost any pride in their past, although their educations were clearly a disaster in light of the reality around them, there might still be a future. Listening to these heartening words, convicts from bad family backgrounds would feel tears come to their eyes.

I was one of those who sincerely admired the Old Commissar. He was different from the other leaders with whom I had come in contact, men who appeared profound but didn't have a thing inside. Every word he spoke seemed spontaneous and new. My remaining vestiges of poetic sensitivity told me that he was truly an artist. He was a model leader among workers-peasants-and-soldiers. I'd heard him give a number of reports, usually just after I had drunk grass soup and didn't feel quite as hungry as usual, and eventually I had the idea of writing about him. After all, didn't I have a pen?

Moreover, it was clear to me that some people were receiving special treatment. Certain convicts did nothing but easy jobs. Since envy was unpleasant, it occurred to me that I too should belong to the ranks of those looked after. I have never been athletic, even when I was younger. By this time there were only forty-four kilos of me left, and I was even less nimble. I was no match against others when it came to eating greens, and when it came to hard labour I was never going to surpass the rest. I had to avoid that path if I wanted to preserve my own little life. Most people are smart enough to display their better side and to hide their faults. I knew that the only usefulness I had was the ability to write. That was the one pitifully meagre talent I had learned in the world Outside. If one was to write in this labour reform camp, the ideal scenario was to make this Old Commissar the main character. I decided to write an article that sang his praises and extolled his virtue. Never mind that he truly *was* worth writing about.

One day, after the Old Commissar had finished his lesson, I bravely marched up and gave a Troop Leader under him a message, describing this aspiration.

Nobody ever gave me an answer, nobody declared any position on it, but several days later the Troop Leader suddenly plucked me out of the Main Work Troop. He said that I was not to go with the rest of the men to the big fields. Instead, I was to do the work that these first entries in the diary mention, good jobs like hauling dirt clods and picking through greens. It was clear that I had been elevated to the status of being looked after.

And so, it became imperative that I use my free time, when I was not hauling clods or picking through greens, to throw myself into writing with all the grateful fervour I could muster. Since I was much more practised at writing than at hauling, I had the article written within a few nights.

By now, I had already begun to correct my final draft.

13 July
Dismantled kang in Duckshed, finished 'Shine On, Crimson Rays'.

*T*he Duckshed was originally on a peninsula at the edge of the lake. That was where it had first been built by the Old Commissar and the dozen cadres he brought in at the start of the camp. It could be considered the camp's earliest piece of capital construction.

At the beginning, they did indeed keep ducks at this place, and there were still a few mouth-watering ducks around, but mainly what lived inside the Duckshed now were convicts. Duck-raising had become a sideline – almost all the convicts worked in the fields raising crops.

In the authorized documents, this place was counted as a Station in the camp, but people still called it the Duckshed. No doubt the name will go on for ever, even when the ducks have long since been eaten, like a lot of place names in China that once had some real meaning.

The peninsula too had changed – it had become a small hill on a marshy sweep of land. From the Duckshed, one became aware of the Old Commissar's vision – you could see why he rejected everyone else's opinion and decided to set up a farm here. Back then, the whole area was a lake, including the labour reform camp and all that surrounded it. The water was deep blue and so clear you could see the bottom. Reeds along the marshy perimeter grew several metres high. According to old-timers, back then foot-long grass-carp would jump straight out of the water and land up on the bank. The pigs that local farmers raised stayed by the shores of the lake just waiting for such fish to eat.

The Old Commissar had made his decision, however, and he declared, 'A place that can grow grass is a place that can grow crops!' Convicts started shouldering baskets of earth, carrying them one by one from a distant place. Slowly they filled in the lake. It is impossible to calculate how many cubic square metres of land had to be transported, basketful by basketful, on the backs of men, in order to fill a lake that once covered such a large area.

A small part of the lake remains today, and the scene is still lovely. When a summer breeze blows across the water, the reeds whisper to one another, and the wind over what remains of the natural lake accompanies them with an echo, like an old woman chanting in a low voice. At noon, a heavy fog rises and the calls of water birds reverberate over the water's mirror-like surface. The occasional water bird spreads his wings and takes off, then settles on top of the forest of reeds after circling like the sound of a song. The sight of it takes convicts back in their thoughts to another world.

But if you disregard scenery that galvanizes the emotions, that grips the bowels, and use a practical eye to assess this natural beauty (beauty so like the famous watery landscapes of southern China), then you might be able to conceive of the possibility of bringing men to this place to build a large-scale state farm.

When convicts first started to haul dirt on their backs and build fields here, it was impossible to produce any grain. Fish and ducks were the only things they could raise to eat. People from northern Shaanxi don't like fish, and they don't know how to raise them. Ducks are different. Ducks taste good and are simple to feed: you herd the flock down to the lake at the start of a day and that's about it. At night, the ducks come home voluntarily on their own. Plus you have the added benefit of a lot of duck eggs. The Old Commissar decided that first they would raise ducks here.

The sun was high by the time I sauntered slowly down to the Duckshed from where I lived. I went all by myself. At least for now, for the present, for this *moment*, I was a convict who could be trusted. I wanted to use this wonderful moment to the utmost. I gazed out over the scenery of the lake along the way as long as I wanted to, even as I tried to ascertain if there was something around to eat. If my luck was good, who's to say, I might run into a local villager on the road. I still had a few coins in my pocket – perhaps I could buy some potatoes.

Most of the buildings comprising the Duckshed were, of course, ducksheds. They were even more primitive than the clod-pile (*gandalei*) I lived in. They had only three walls – the open side had a kind of gate made of reeds. It blocked the rain, but not the wind. Although it reeked of duck shit inside, the air was actually quite fresh. The main drawback to living there was that it was only about one and a half metres tall. You had to do everything bent over at the waist, except when you lay down to sleep.

Since it had originally had ducks living in it, and since people could not sleep directly on the damp, shitty ground, they had built kangs* inside for the convicts. Getting on and off the kang was like pulling out a drawer – you pushed yourself in and pulled yourself out. Today, I worked as assistant to a big worker. I helped him dismantle the dirt clods of a kang and move them out into the yard – it was summer now and the bed was unnecessary, so the clods could be better used as fertilizer.

*A kind of platform bed.

To do this, the big worker and I had to work sitting down. Although it was inconvenient, it was actually quite comfortable. I thought it strange that they should order me to do such a simple job. Could they not have had a convict who actually lived in the Duckshed do it?

'You can't trust a convict from the Duckshed,' the big worker told me. 'Hell, they're all thieves. If you let them stay at home, that'd be the end of all the ducks and duck eggs.' When he said 'home', he meant these ducksheds, and specifically the narrow kangs or bunks that the convicts slept on. Most of the convicts in the Duckshed Station were those who had committed real crimes, and this kind of person was 'unreliable'.

I had been here for over seven hundred days, and knew quite well that men in this world and on the Outside were judged by different standards. In the outside world the most unreliable men, namely political convicts, were the ones who were considered most dependable here in the camps. Rightists, historical counter-revolutionaries and all kinds of 'thought criminals' did not dare escape, did not dare talk back, did not dare be disobedient or make trouble. With criminal convicts, it was the opposite – it was impossible to change their old habits.

This big worker was a camp employee, a freed convict who had stayed on after his term of imprisonment was completed. Although he had served his sentence and was nominally a normal human being, he was still regarded as a 'released-convict-from-labour-reform-and-labour-education'. One could never peel off the skin of a convict, even after getting out. He was around forty, with a strong physique, so it looked as though he had some way of supplementing the insufficiencies of his grain ration. After working for a while, I began to realize from what he said that he must be rather highly regarded by the leaders. This was because he was capable of doing just about any kind of work, and he could be trusted. He was one of the convicts in the first batch that came to the camp. As soon as he arrived he was noticed by the Old Commissar, who assigned him to the kitchen to be a cook. I asked him how he had been so lucky.

'The Old Commissar knew what was what!' he smiled. He spoke in a thick Hunan accent. 'He had seen the verdict on me. I had been an orderly for a regimental commander – so I never actually fought against the Liberation Army on a battleground. Then too I was from a poor farming background. So I knew how to work, had an eye for it.

'You see, you scamp, having an eye for what to do is much more important than simply having a back for the work. That's something you'd better remember. You, for instance, haven't got it. You've piled up all the clods right there in the doorway – in a minute we won't be able to get out!'

I told him that I wasn't strong enough to throw the clods further into the yard – I just couldn't do it.

He looked me over for a moment, and then said, with great pity, 'You're a man of ink and letters, culture – I can see that. When they serve the next meal, I'll get the cook to give you a little extra.'

With this encouragement, I threw the dismantled clods as far as I could, then piled them up until I was exhausted.

At noon, when it was time to eat, there was no sight of him. This Kuomintang bastard, this historical counter-revolutionary bum! He had gone off by himself to the workers-and-peasants mess hall to eat, without remembering his promise.

I stared hard at the kitchen help serving the food. I widened my eyes at them, hoping that he might have left them a word. Maybe they would recognize me from his description. But the kitchen staff were indifferent. They gave me the same as the other convicts, pouring exactly one ladle of thin soup into my bowl.

As I sat alone on top of the clods I had thrown from the duckshed, sullenly finishing my watery soup, he came sauntering back, full and belching. He pulled two duck eggs from the pockets of his trousers.

'These are for you,' he said. 'Cooked and ready. Enjoy!'

I was astounded. I had never imagined good fortune could drop so suddenly on my head. And the manner in which he bestowed these alms on me was that of the most gracious multi-millionaire. Nowadays, is it possible for a man to appear so rich?

I ate one egg, savouring it as though I had never eaten such a delicious thing in my life. First, with regret, I removed the shell, which really was inedible. Then I carefully wrapped the other egg in the cloth I used to wipe off sweat with, and stashed it for the time being under the eaves of the duckshed. I was afraid I might crush it as I worked if I left it in my pocket.

'Eat it!' he said. 'How could one be enough?!'

'No, it's enough . . . just about enough.' That's one good thing about intellectuals: they look at things with an analytical mind, even when it comes to eating. A duck egg is small enough to just about fit in the mouth whole, but if you think of the calories, the protein, the fat, one egg should be enough to satisfy the needs of the whole body.

In the afternoon, we became very friendly. He told me that he had been sentenced in 1953. Not long after the rebellion of his regiment, his commander was captured and the troops under the commander were put together to form a 'study group'. They were asked to expose the crimes of their leader. Those who didn't expose enough were to be 'legally' dealt with. Not a single man reached the standard of 'enough'. He said his sentence was regarded as light: only five years.

'In fact, those five years were better than being back home!' he said with some satisfaction. 'I ate duck every day: could I ever do that when I was with the KMT?'

'Do you still eat duck now?' There was considerable envy in my voice.

'Of course! Whatever the Old Commissar eats, I eat too.' He smiled as he explained, 'Those Shaanbei people don't know what to do with a duck. They boil it in plain old water and eat it, and call it duck! Ridiculous. We Hunanese really know how to cook it. Soy-sauced duck, salty-water duck, steamed duck, phoenix duck. I can even make pressed duck. The Old Commissar only likes to eat duck cooked by me.'

'The Old Commissar is eating duck now too?' I was shocked. I couldn't imagine, with the entire country starving, that the Commissar I so respected would not share the sweet and the bitter alike with his people.

'Of course! One a day! You think he's going to give *you* a duck to eat that he raises for himself? Ha!' He derided me on behalf of the Old Commissar.

This had to be simple blasphemy against the Old Commissar. From the look on the man's face, though, it was clear that he didn't see anything wrong in the Commissar's eating duck that belonged to us all every day. He seemed quite nonchalant about it, which was the reason he dared to say it out loud.

We intellectuals are different. When we know that something isn't right, we know we shouldn't talk about it. What's more, we dare not talk about it. Those who do the thinking for leaders like the Old Commissar are often mistaken about which opponents to be on guard against. The ones they should worry about are those who have no concept of ethics, not intellectuals, who are only too clear about which things can be said and which can't. Despite this, the Old Commissar warned us intellectuals more than anyone. He practically beat our arses off about it every day. But in fact, intellectuals know exactly what can be broadcast and what must be deeply concealed.

Take me, for example. If I had known that the Old Commissar was eating the people's ducks every day, I would have guarded the secret more closely than the Old Commissar himself.

By chance, I had now learned that the Old Commissar was eating duck, but I continued writing the article about him just the same. His image had been somewhat diminished in my mind – nevertheless, I put special emphasis on the old man's honesty in performing his public duties. Chinese intellectuals have always considered it taboo to say anything bad about respected elders and relatives. This tradition fits in neatly with the call by the leaders for literature to 'praise New Men, and praise revolutionary leaders'. It allows writers to feel that they are maintaining a sense of propriety. The system of censorship that we have here is completely unnecessary – writers already have a very strict self-censorship bureau inside their heads.

That evening, I lay on my stomach on my bedding, praising the Old Commissar in 'Shine On, Crimson Rays', and at the same time secretly eating the duck egg that had slipped between his fingers. All in all, it had been a pretty good day. I had not met any local people on the road and had not been able to buy a potato, but instead I had been given something that contains who knows how many times the protein of a potato. I also felt that the article was going smoothly. The title may have been rather vulgar, but it was fashionable for literary titles to be in that style. Compared to other articles that were swelling the magazines right now, such as 'Make Haste to Get in the Autumn Crop', 'Onward, Onward to the Planting!', 'An Abundant Harvest Depends on the Summer and Fall', 'The Party Secretary Stays with his Troop to do the Spring Planting', 'You Are Our Model', 'Nursemaid Pig', etc., 'Shine on, Crimson Rays' at least had some poetry to it.

14 July
Morning dug up wild plants, afternoon picked through them.

I have said above that some convicts behaved irresponsibly when they dug up plants to eat. Today it was my turn. Convicts allowed to dig plants tended to be chosen from among those in the infirmary and those being 'looked after'. When the Main Work Troop went off to work as usual, we were gathered together and taken by a relatively mild Troop Leader to some nearby open land.

At a specified place, we all spread out again, to find the thicker patches of wild plants to dig. We were a little like wild rabbits that have their own range in which to find food. Convicts from the infirmaries did not actually dig. They would find a dry place where the grass was thick and lie down. The Troop Leader didn't much mind even if he saw them – he had his motives. Sick men were supposed to be lying in bed. To get them to come out and round out your numbers was already doing quite well.

We convicts who were being looked after were the ones who really had to dig. The Troop Leader was extremely strict with us. The reason was that we were responsible for digging up enough grass for the entire camp's meal, clump by clump. We were already considered privileged by not having to go out and work in the fields, by not having to endure crazy-itching bumps.

'Every one of you digs twenty-five *jin*.* If you don't make it, you're not going to eat!' The Troop Leader stood

---

*One jin is equal to half a kilogram or 1.1 pounds, so twenty-five jin equals twelve and a half kilos or twenty-seven and a half pounds.

on a high point and yelled down at us. Then he found a dry, cool spot to lie down.

In order to eat my one bowl of thin grass soup, I too dug out weeds and grasses with roots, dirt and all. I was just sorry that the dirt wasn't heavier.

The entire country was supposed to be 'suffering through natural disasters', but somehow the weather where we were, and apparently only where we were, was beautiful. It was hard to understand why nature should be so kindly disposed towards us. The weather was beautiful, but we were starving. In the moment when a clump of grass came out of the ground with a great sucking sound, up would come an earthy fragrance that only loess possesses.* The green vapour of this fragrance was intoxicating, making you feel you were seated at a banquet, or at the very least near a fruit stand. The smell seeped into your lungs, then mixed with your blood and circulated through your body.

Absorbing this earthy green vapour, I felt that my body was expanding and becoming transparent. Maybe it was because I had eaten so much thin grass soup, and my body had already stored a lot of chlorophyll which was merging with the greenness of the world, but for a brief moment I ceased to feel hungry. Instead I felt that I was a tender green leaf, carefree and self-confident.

And indeed, I was only twenty-three. Compared to annuals, plants that come back year after year, that was still fairly young!

The land on either side of the Yellow River has been deposited there by silt flooding down year after year. As

*Loess is fertile soil that has been deposited over this area by wind blowing down from the north-west.

56

a result, the earth on the roots of uprooted plants has layers like the pages of a book. The layers tell their own history. Each shows a passage of time, tells a wondrous story that it is impossible for humans to know or understand. I had never had this sort of contact with the real earth – not the kind of muck that carries rotting plants and stinging salts, the stinking goo that gives you crazy-itching bumps, but this most basic yellow earth. It was earth from which a myriad things could grow, earth that was exactly the same colour as our skin, that had the same smell as our bodies. As I dug grass, I examined it with a very strong emotion. The pages of the book crumpled in my hand, the dry dust of the yellow earth circled around me like a mist as I was introduced to an ancient world. The rustling sound of grass being pulled was like the turning of hand-bound pages of an ancient tome. Both held scholarship that I would never be able to read.

Early-morning sunlight, a slight breeze, moist grassy earth and grasshoppers whirring happily in the green air around me – with a profound and most interesting form of book in my hands, I could temporarily forget my position in life and be moved to write poetry.

But there was a danger in this that could easily lead to tragedy: it was precisely because of my dog-shitting poems that I was doing hard labour. China has an old saying: 'Mountains and rivers are easy to move, but it's impossible to change a man's nature.' Even if I had wanted not to write poems, poetry seemed to wrap itself around me.

Nothing unfortunate happened this day, however. From the diary entry, it seems I was able to eat my bowl of grass soup. I was not punished by being denied a meal, and, even better, in the afternoon I was told to do my favourite job, picking through greens.

None the less, I can guarantee that I did not complete the assigned task. Twenty-five jin is not a small quantity. If you don't believe it, try digging that amount with your own two hands, and on an empty stomach. A certain percentage of what I dug I ate.

15 July
Rest. Manuscript sealed, but not mailed. Afternoon listened to report (Station Leader Wang, Division Leader Hou, Old Commissar). Began Double-Counter.

*T*here was no established system for 'rest' in the labour reform camp, no regular day off. But even machines need to be checked over and repaired occasionally. At times of the year when there was less farmwork to do, the leaders would pick a time when they thought it would be all right for us not to go to work and they would allow us not to go to work. This sentence sounds awkward, but there isn't a better way of putting it. You will find similar sentences in what follows. A new set of social circumstances has to produce a new semantic structure.

It could not be called resting, so it was called not going to work. Such days were actually harder, especially for people like me who were being looked after. Convicts who worked in the big fields also disliked not going to work. The main reason was that not going to work meant that the camp provided only two meals: one at nine in the morning and another at four in the afternoon. Try and find a way to make one bowl of grass soup last that long in your stomach!

As a result, the most important activity on such days was to look everywhere for something to eat. We were not allowed to go out into the open land to look, though. Like ghostly shadows moving on two thin legs, convicts would move back and forth in a circumscribed area. Like ants passing one another, ear to ear, they would all be foraging for food.

You had to scrutinize each man's expression. A convict's glance might be a signal, and this signal, like ants nudging one another, might be telling you that near by there was something to eat. Understanding this, you and

61

he would go off to a corner to talk. The most common form the business took was barter. There was no standard of value. The transaction depended entirely on the wishes of the two parties. This was actually quite fair and equitable – it had to bring satisfaction to both sides.

My Longines watch, for example, was traded for ten local grain coupons. My Italian briefcase was exchanged for five bowls of black noodles. A woollen Sun Yatsen jacket was traded for a pack of tobacco laced with sawdust, a tie was traded for a radish. (The old man was delighted with my tie – he was going to use it as a belt to hold his pants up. He said over and over how durable it was.) No one forced me to make an exchange at these prices. I felt that every one of them was just about right.

Like any market, the market in the convicts' compound also had rudimentary ethics. If you saw two people squatting beside the dirt wall talking softly to each other, as an honourable man you wouldn't walk over and interfere. That was a transaction being consummated. You could stand to one side, however, so that if the parties did not agree one or the other of them would know to try you next. There were some active traders with a knack for this kind of business – either they had the backing of nearby families, who would send things to them regularly, or they were agents for free convicts, like the cooks or those who drove the trucks or raised the livestock. They might even be agents for some of the cadres.* With such men making a market, so long as you had things to trade you could always be confident of trading them for something to eat.

Every intellectual owns a watch. When the first con-

*Government employees who ran the camps.

victs came into the camp, they had to hand over these watches to the authorities. The leaders in charge told them that they wouldn't need to know the time any more. This seemed a reasonable explanation for the confiscation. After a while, though, the regulation was not so strictly adhered to. The reason was that there were too many people being sent to the camp. It was like that phrase, 'When there are too many radishes, you don't wash off the dirt.' It was also like customs officers checking foreigners during the height of tourist season: when the crowds surge through, they hardly glance at a passport before going on to the next.

Consequently, the labour reform camp became the only source of supply for watches in the area. In addition to watches, there were a number of excellent things that the local people had never seen – and the price was dirt cheap. There is nothing more valuable than life to men on the verge of dying. This was the reason we were so frantically busy on days when we did 'not go to work'.

Neighbouring villagers, workers in the local farms and cadres among the authorities of the labour reform camp, as well as their relatives, all looked for agents to do their work. They wanted people who could carry on a good trade with the convicts. These brokers received benefits from both sides of the business. They were regarded as upper-crust among the criminals. Since they always had things to eat, they had more energy than a common convict with which to do their work. If you had something to sell and needed something to eat right away, your best chance was to look for a convict the leaders had been praising recently as a 'good performer'.

During the few days I was being looked after, I could eat grass any time I wanted. I did not have to search for food, and so I could lounge at home, dreaming up poetry. Like Pushkin in exile, leaning against the rocks at Odessa, I lay on my stomach on the bedding. Perhaps he absent-mindedly watched the seagulls soaring above; I silently watched convicts carrying things as they moved back and forth. Some were excited, some depressed. It was not an easy thing to score at this bartering business – clever convicts generally had several meetings with someone before coming to a deal.

According to convention, we were never given the entire day 'off'. The authorities of the camp would use half a day administering education to the convicts. Today was no exception. People were hurriedly finishing trading what they had to trade – the pay-off hadn't yet reached their stomachs – when we heard the piercing sound of the whistle.

'All gather at the threshing ground – now!'

I use the term threshing ground, but in fact this square was used for many purposes. It was an athletic field, where cadres played badminton or basketball or did calisthenics to a loudspeaker, and it was an open-air theatre for movies. It was a small park where cadres' families would knit as they gossiped, and it was a place used to assemble the convicts for general meetings. When the crops were in, however, after spring and autumn harvest, all activities made way for the grain. So the name 'threshing ground' is still appropriate.

The convicts were swiftly led to the square from their Numbers. There they lined up neatly according to their groups, and then sat down together under the blazing sun. Until the leaders arrived, some might do a little sewing. Many convicts brought along clothes that needed interminable mending – everyone had become a pro at patching. Convicts who had been eating well, that is the high-class convicts, took the opportunity to look over the best specimens among the female convicts. What I remember most about that wait, though, something that I have not forgotten to this day, was the pervasive sound of coughing.

Have you ever heard more than one thousand people coughing hard at the same time? It was an intense, wild coughing, an explosive sound erupting uncontrollably from unhealthy lungs. It was like the crashing of ocean waves coming in from a distance, one wave always higher than the next. Especially during late rollcall on a winter night, the coughing could almost make the freezing air shiver. You simply could not believe that the ear-splitting sound was coming from the human respiratory system. It was more like glass being shattered. Some coughs were low and suppressed, others resounded, some were extended, others short barks. Some were accompanied by phlegm, others were a dry rasping that wouldn't stop. It was as though every animal in a forest had simultaneously begun to roar.

I have never seen this bone-chilling collective coughing described in any book about concentration camps or prisons. Either it has never occurred before, or writers have disregarded it. I remember it so vividly myself mainly because I was a part of it. The weather was scorchingly hot and dry on this summer day in July of 1960. I felt that the lobes of my lungs had become as thin as paper, that they could no longer stand to have gas inside, going in and out. Every breath made them more fragile and tremulous. Naturally I was an active participant in the chorus.

All convicts, however, myself included, are despicable.

No sooner would the leaders appear and stand majest-
ically before us than the coughing would immediately
stop. It was as though someone had issued an order and
the ocean waves all hit a reef. It is clear that the conscious
mind plays a large role in controlling a person's body. As
soon as the nerves tighten, sickness seems to disappear.

One after another, the leaders of the labour reform
camp then gave us a lecture. My description of their
lectures in the diary is brief – besides my limited energy
and my instinct to use fewer words to write more, the
reason is basically that the leaders' lectures were all
the same. With only minor differences, they would repeat
themselves ad infinitum. It was incredibly tedious, so I
felt that writing down the main points of the talks was
enough. Today, all three leaders said we had to launch
a 'Double-Counter Movement'.

After listening intently, we found out that 'double-
counter' meant countering, i.e. going against, bad people
and bad things. Without saying so specifically, the sharp
spearhead of this movement was again aimed straight
at us. And not just those of us who had already come
in, we bad people who were already convicts. The outside world was also engaged in double-countering.
Indeed, on the Outside they were clearly already hard
at it. I now understood why the labour reform camp was
so actively building new buildings: it was preparing to
receive new guests.

Each of the three leaders gave the message in his own
way. Station Leader Wang was a middle-aged, tall, thin
man with fair skin – he looked a bit like an intellectual.
He slowly and deliberately laid out the absolute neces-
sity of this new movement for us. He even quoted Chen
Boda.

'Comrade Boda says, "Marxism-Leninisim teaches us that the dictatorship of the proletariat is not the end of class struggle. It is the continuation of another form of class struggle. If the capitalist system has not yet been completely obliterated in the world, if classes have not been wiped out and the influence of capitalist thinking still exists, then there will still be class struggle. The capitalist class will use this class struggle as a means to fight against our socialist revolution. It will use every weapon it can to destroy socialist construction." '

It had been a long time since I had heard this kind of bookish language. Clearly, Station Leader Wang had come with a prepared speech. His cadences were well modulated, his intonation was perfect, he had even memorized the punctuation – his recitation was flawless. Chinese intellectuals worship this kind of book-talk, especially words that have been written by someone of prestige and standing. When the words of Authorities are quoted by leaders, they have an even greater power to intimidate people.

Criminal convicts and the historical counter-revolutionaries among us were not affected by this speech. Those who were mending kept on mending; those who were flirting with the female convicts kept on flirting. But rightists and other thought-offenders felt that there was really something to it. The lesson used a process of logical deduction that every convict who had committed so-called political crimes had used himself in the past. We had all reasoned that way before – never mind that by now we had lost the ability to think.

The train of logical thinking in our minds had been severed – accepting the speech chapter and verse, we all now decided that we should 'counter' ourselves, as well as all those other bad people out there. We should fight against all those who opposed socialist revolution and wished to destroy socialist construction.

Unlike a cream-filled cookie, the filling in a general meeting was always the least interesting. Not a word of what Division Leader Hou had to say deserves mention. But the Old Commissar was different. He described the Double-Counter Movement to his audience with the acute sensitivity of a politician. Departing from his normal practice, he began by quoting a line frequently seen in the newspaper: 'The East Wind has now flattened the West Wind, the situation is excellent!'

This 'East Wind has flattened the West Wind' was a phrase the Great Chairman Mao had used in Moscow the previous year. It was still fresh to our ears. He first quoted this and other phrases to pre-empt any doubts we might be feeling.

'The situation is excellent, yet there are still *bad people*! The Yellow River has a bottom but people's hearts are fathomless! When the woods get big, they attract all kinds of birds! Those who eat gourds can also eat stinky bugs! . . .'

He strung together three lively proverbs that had originated in old folk sayings. They were the distillation of thousands of years of peasant experience. We all nodded in agreement – how true! Society is complex: how could there be no discontented souls at all, even with the best government in the world? It was absolutely vital to go against these bad people and bad things.

Intellectuals felt a small drum beating inside as they listened: where was the 'bottom' of their own hearts? Was this bottom standing securely on the foundation of the proletariat, the propertyless class? One would never want to be a person whose heart could not be seen through to, who was suspect. And what kind of a bird could one be considered? A bad bird among the branches, or a good bird? Worst of all, could one possibly be considered a stinky bug?

16 July
Picked through greens, plan to mail manuscript by 18th at latest. 'In praise of the Municipal People's Commune' and 'Train' to be sent to *Stars*, 'Shine on, Crimson Rays' to be sent to *Ningxia News*. Wrote Mama a letter, will mail 17th.

*D*espite the fervour with which the three leaders reported the launching of the Double-Counter Movement, not much happened for a while. Little action was taken in the labour reform camp. Criminal convicts were already considered bad people, so their attitude was: 'The bigger the debts the less you need to worry, the more the lice the less time you should waste scratching them.'

The mental burden on intellectual convicts had been increased, but all they could do was await their fate. Their future was in the hands of the gods. It appears from this day's diary entry that while the Main Work Troop went out to work as usual, I was still being looked after by being assigned to pick through greens.

The speeches of the leaders had taken so long the previous afternoon that the time for evening mess came and went. The kitchen staff couldn't just say to the Old Commissar, 'Your time's up! Meal's served!' Instead they had to wait until the entire lesson was over before serving. As a result, our stomachs had already passed beyond hunger – we didn't really feel like eating. I heard our Group Leader making his report afterwards when all the Group Leaders were called in for a meeting. 'After hearing the leaders' speeches,' he said, 'everyone was high on the leaders' words. They had such passionate discussions they entirely forgot about eating. From now on, we have to give them more of this sort of spiritual sustenance.' This

71

kind of thing was how a Group Leader got to be a Group Leader.*

With my stomach recently stuffed full of wild plants, I apparently retrieved the inspiration that had evaporated for a while. Taking advantage of it, I wrote two 'poems'. Although somewhat deflated by the news from the KMT man in the Duckshed that the Old Commissar was eating duck every day (so that when he was up there talking about countering bad people all I could hear below was quacking), I was still planning to submit 'Shine on, Crimson Rays'.

In addition to those with essential abilities in the camp, such as doctors, people with professional skills would receive special treatment from time to time. These included filmmakers, painters, musicians, actors, singers, etc. I was not the only one to be taken care of simply because I could write. There were quite a few 'pens' among the cadres of the state farm who could be used to produce 'attack material' – material used to incriminate and damage others. It was unclear why I had been called on this time. Maybe the Old Commissar wanted to have a convict, as opposed to a cadre, writing good things about him. Maybe he knew why I had become a convict and he wanted to test me. Considering it might be the latter, it was necessary that I polish the article until it couldn't be better.

Once you set pen to paper, it's hard to stop – this is another bad habit that writers find it hard to resist. The two poems 'Praising the Municipal People's Commune'

*A Group Leader was a convict in charge of other convicts. Such a man enjoyed certain benefits by playing up to Troop Leaders, who were not convicts.

and 'Train' could be called subsidiary works to 'Shine on, Crimson Rays'. I'm not proud of them as poetry, but in the course of writing them I suddenly found the knack of writing poetry during those years in China. I understood how those poets who were often praised by the leaders wrote their work.

The trick could be summed up by the phrase 'borrowing a body to put your soul in'. No matter what inspiration poets got from nature, life, love, anything that sparked a passionate response, the result had to be neatly redirected to some leader who was to be praised. Artistic sentiments could certainly be expressed – they just had to be associated with someone it was permissible to extol. For example, memories of one's mother, or love for one's mother, had to be changed to love for the Party. Anything to do with the sun, or moon, or glorious sunrises, in fact all of Nature's rays of light, had to be applied to the Great Chairman Mao Zedong. Light could be used only to describe him. Any tender emotions born of feelings for a young woman, or a lover, were best applied to lauding the achievements of textile workers, or female tractor drivers. Poetic sensitivity might be graced with the most exquisite sentences, with what is often called divine inspiration, but the poet had better bestow that inspiration on something to do with a hydroelectric plant. Modern farming equipment, a steel furnace, a lathe etc. would also do. My poem 'Train' is an example. All of these came under the rubric 'New Things Produced by Socialism'.

Without this device, you would have no place to express your poetic impulse, and it would slowly disappear from your mind. You might truly wish to extol the Party, praise the Great Leader Chairman Mao, sing

73

the praises of textile workers and female tractor drivers, praise hydroelectric plants, steel furnaces, lathes and so forth – and it is true that there are poets who have now grown up in the New Society who have this kind of political fervour. But don't be foolish – you cannot derive poetic feeling from such things alone. You still have to be inspired by people and events that have an intimate relationship to your life. You repackage these, and put them to use extolling some object that has a political nature.

When you have done this, not only does your poem meet a political standard, dictated by the guiding principle that 'Literature must serve the needs of politics', but it also contains some poetry. Otherwise, it will be nothing but a string of slogans. I believe that, starting with the Great Proletarian Poet Mayakovsky, socialist poetry has been written in this way.

With this realization, I appreciated the fact that many modern Chinese poets write eulogies of the leaders in order to exercise their emotions; they don't write poetry in order to eulogize. It's the same as not caring what kind of receptacle you use when you are relieving yourself.

Who the devil knows why the Municipal People's Commune was significant? And yet here I was writing a poem to praise it. The phrase must have been something I had seen in a newspaper. It was probably the result of the cities following the good example of the villages. Villages were plunging vigorously into communization. All property owned by farmers was being given over to the public, to everyone. Families slowly dissolved as everyone was required to go to a common mess hall to eat. The principle of dividing everything into equal shares took hold. Watching this principle in action, city people were unhappy to be left behind: they too wanted to join this thing called 'philosophy of communal property', namely Communism, right away.

It was said that the glorious prospect of the future was that all China would become one large commune. You could go anywhere to eat and you wouldn't need to pay any money. Money itself would be eradicated. Then people could put their minds to getting on with things and not worry about it. This idea nicely matched ideas of Confucius that I had been exposed to and influenced by since my childhood. Confucius espoused the ideal of *datong* – literally 'big together' or, more poetically, 'great harmony'.

The loftiest ideals are always the most abstract, but right now they were tied to things in which I was passionately interested. They had to do with the most basic desires, such as 'going anywhere to eat and not having to pay any money for it'. So it wasn't unreasonable for me to sing the praises of these ideals. Indeed, there were some pretty decent sentences in the poem, inspired by when I was digging grass or picking through weeds.

Still, it was surprising that I was moved to write poetry. People were dying one after another in front of my eyes, dying right next to me, yet I still raised my voice in song. Famine not only took countless lives, it also murdered countless poems. If I had been able to eat to my fill, I could certainly have written thousands of eulogies.

But what best expressed my personal emotions was the letter I wrote to my mother. I was no more than a tender green sprout. When it came to my mother, I would never grow up, so that even in such a proper, careful diary, I was still calling out, 'Mama!'

17 July
Picked through greens, gave two manuscripts and letter for mother to Li Guoliang to mail from Station Three.
18 July
Picked through greens.
19 July
Morning dug grass – eighteen jin, afternoon picked through greens.
20 July
Moved to Main Camp, afternoon hauled dirt clods (25).

*T*he future is opaque. It is impossible for any person to know his fate, but this was especially true of convicts. One moment you might be doing one job, and then suddenly you'd be transferred somewhere else.

I had been enjoying the comforts of 'being looked after', I had sent my article and two poems off with a man who would mail them for me, when I was told to move out of my 'home'. We were moving to the Main Camp.

I would take a tattered piece of cloth, also that small glass bottle I had. A piece of thread, for who was to say when I might need it – labour reform convicts hated to part with anything other than snot and phlegm. The cleanest part of a labour reform camp was the garbage pile. You wouldn't find anything there that could be put to use somewhere else. When we were ready, each man shouldered his baggage and left, leaving nothing but a foul odour behind in the barracks.

The diary entries of the preceding days were written at Station Four. The organization of all the Stations of the camp was the same, the only distinction being that some were extremely primitive, and others not quite so primitive. Station Four was in the first category, the Main Camp was in the second. Except for that, there was nothing else worth emphasizing here. The Main Camp was made up of row after row of buildings in a large compound, surrounded by an earthen wall which had a large wooden gate. Each earthen building was divided into a number of barracks – as mentioned earlier, these were known as Numbers. That was about it.

The problem was that after being moved I lost my

protection. I lost my status of being looked after. I wondered if the Old Commissar would remember me and pass on any instructions to the leaders here. Since we moved to the Main Camp in the morning and that afternoon I was assigned to haul dirt clods, it looked as though the Old Commissar had not said anything to anyone.

By then, the policy of 'lowered-rations-to-be-substituted-with-gourds-and-greens' had already been in effect for more than a year. Those who were close to dying had already died; those who hadn't died were now in the process. People were going rapidly in succession. In the end, whether or not one would die depended on fate. Would I die? I had no way of knowing. I knew only that the weakness and exhaustion of my body was something I had never seen described in any work of literature, from Qu Yuan* and Homer all the way down to today. I won't repeat what I have already written about that, but I want to add one point. Every moment, twenty-for hours a day, I had to be aware that I must not forget to breathe.

The respiratory system is controlled by the automatic nervous system. It functions on its own, breathing away, no matter whether one is conscious or not. At that point in my life, however, it was necessary for me to work the system consciously. If I forgot to breathe, there was a danger of suffocating. This problem was not a result of some illness of the central respiratory system, nor was it caused by injury to the head or lung disease. The fatigue of my body had simply led to an exhaustion of my lungs, as though they too were too worn out to work. At first,

*Chinese poet of the fourth century BC.

I often did forget to breathe and found that I would suddenly be dizzy, with pricks of light behind my eyes. Darkness would rise up before me as I fell over. Later I became accustomed to remembering to take in oxygen.

Gradually, only two things of any importance remained in my life: eating grass soup and breathing.

The miracle was that I could still move, could still work, by eating only grass soup and breathing air. I even discovered that compared to others I was still fairly strong. This impressed me with the fact that I was a live man, not a near-dead one, and this in turn fired my will to live. Many who were weaker than I were also still living, and this too was an incentive – it provoked me to carry on.

It would not be quite right to say that those who died had died of starvation, since every day each convict got at least three bowls of grass soup. Because of a gradual weakening, though, people slowly atrophied. This gave them more time to think about it than a sudden death. By then, people looked as though they suffered from the 'withering syndrome' that plants get. In plants this is because certain bacteria, such as Fusarium, Verticullium, Pseudomonas etc., enter the roots and stalks and then arrest their vascular bundles. The circulation system becomes blocked up or poisoned by bacteria and other organisms, so that plants gradually stop functioning normally. This leads to a withering phenomenon and an inability to regain good health. Applied to humans, it exhibits itself in a kind of 'death mask'.

Needless to say, men with such death masks were emaciated. In addition, the skin of their faces and entire bodies turned a dull, dark colour; their hair looked dried-out and scorched; the mucous of their eyes increased but the eyes themselves became exceedingly, strangely bright. They emitted a 'thief's glare', a kind of shifty, scared and yet crafty, debilitated but also poisonous light. No one felt afraid when they saw it though, for they knew that their own eyes were not much different.

Can you comprehend just how weak this condition made a man? Imagine a single stem of rice on the ground – now imagine being unable to lift your leg when you want to step over it.

Some developed oedema. It began first in the feet, then spread quickly to the calves, then the entire lower limbs until it reached the head. The person soon resembled a balloon that has been filled full of air – the eyes would swell so that they became small slits: light couldn't penetrate them and one could not see out. But simple, straightforward oedema could still not be described as a death mask. If the skin on the part that was swelling began to split and a yellow glandular fluid oozed out, then death was not far away.

People in our group began to die one after another. If you got up in the morning and discovered that the person beside you had died, the thing to do was make a report to the Group Leader in the following manner: 'Group Leader, So-and-so has died.' Whatever happened, you never wanted to say, 'Oh! Group Leader, another person has died!' This subtle linguistic difference is something that people who were not in the camps in the 1960s cannot understand.

The ones who could tell the linguistic distinction between these two phrases were, quite naturally, intellectuals. If you said 'another', an intellectual convict would immediately take hold of your 'speech-handle' – something you might have said that could be grabbed on to and used against you. If it was handled lightly, the informant would make a report to the Troop Leader. If it was more severe, then the Authorities would institute criticism.

'You said "another" person has died! What's that supposed to mean? If a man has died, he's died, why should you insist on adding "another"? Isn't that smearing black on us, slandering the situation of everyone here? Why do you pay attention to another dead person, and not to another person who has been properly reformed?

'You were wearing rose-tinted glasses on the Outside. You picked at the dark side of socialism, and now you're here doing labour reform and still not changing your old ways. What do you have to say for yourself? What did you mean? Were you intentionally trying to stir up discontent among the convicts? Well? Speak! Were you?'

You had to forget all about the man who had died beside you right away. Next time, when 'another' died, you had to think of him as the first. It was necessary to get accustomed to this method of accounting, for no matter how many died in the camps, they were all the only one who died.

The way intellectual convicts treated other intellectual convicts was often more cruel than the behaviour of the Troop Leaders. A Troop Leader could only discern if a convict was working fast or slow, and, when he worked, whether or not he was putting all his strength into it. Intellectuals, on the other hand, could hear the innuendoes in the most subtle distinctions of language. If a Troop Leader was displeased with a convict, even the most barbaric would just hit him and kick him, or order another criminal convict to come and do it for him. If there were more to be done then it would be the photograph treatment. But the Authorities in the camps did not understand that intellectual convicts were singularly unafraid of being kicked or beaten. What they feared was words and written criticism.

After being hit for a while, an intellectual convict would crawl up from the ground, shake off the dust and go on as though nothing had happened. But if he had been given a verbal and written critique, his soul would feel as wounded as though he had been severely stabbed. For days on end he would not be able to raise his head, to the point that he would lose any interest in staying alive. This was because every intellectual convict had scars on his heart that had not healed over. Six years later, during the Cultural Revolution, quantities of evidence showed that many intellectuals were more terrified of criticism than they were of death.

Criminal convicts were also afraid of criticism, but they had a special means of dealing with those who criticized them. If an intellectual convict criticized someone . . . fine, let's just see when it comes time to work!

'Fucker! You filthy traitorous bastard. When the chance comes, damned if I don't get you singled out for attack till you're dead!'

How would he 'single the man out for attack'? In addition to what I have already written above, about a criminal convict's describing every conceivable posture of making love with his criticizer's mother, also laying out both her physical beauties and defects in broad daylight, a more severe way was to make sure he was the one to pack the intellectual's hauling basket.

These criminal convicts too were not much more than a hungry rack of bones. But they had been born to work, and they could lift a heavy load of dirt in one shovelful. If you were on good terms with the man, he would lift it high over the hauling basket on your back and set it in gently.

'How's that? Like scratching a little itch, right?'

But if you had angered him, or criticized him . . . sorry! He would lift the shovelful of dirt high and ruthlessly smash it down. 'I'll teach you to sell your mouth, you dogshitter!' There was no way language criticism could outdo shovel criticism.

Back in the small-group meetings, the more courageous criticizers would be kicked to a kneeling position on the ground. If you got off easy that would mean the dog-eating-mud treatment. A more severe punishment and the discs between your vertebrae would start to protrude.

Then there were criminal convicts who neither cursed nor smashed down with their iron shovels, but who made sure you never got to eat the packages that your family might have sent. One came, it was stolen; two came, both were stolen. And if the intellectual's stinking mouth dared to challenge this, the criminal convict would crack open lips that were greasy from your stolen food and laugh.

Since intellectual convicts were not afraid to die, they made up the largest number of those who did die. As soon as a criminal convict had the slightest feeling that his body was not up to working, he would lie down and refuse to work. The most ruthless of Troop Leaders had no way to deal with this practice of 'pretending to be a dead dog' and sleeping all day at 'home'. He could only say regretfully, 'A good man fears a lazy one, a lazy man fears a wastrel, but a wastrel fears someone who doesn't care about face!'

This apt proverb expressed our traditional rules of restraint among people. As soon as a person doesn't care about face, even Yan Wang, King of Hell, has to regard him as beyond hope. Intellectuals care about face. They were also aware of the fact that they were different from criminal convicts. Criminal convicts had brought harm to the people, and so were considered 'internal-contra-dictions-among-the-people', but intellectuals were some-thing much worse. They were 'contradictions-between-the-people-and-the enemy'.

Stranger than this peculiar kind of logic was the fact that intellectual convicts actually believed it. They were quite willing to accept that they belonged to a lower class than criminal convicts, to believe that no matter how bad criminal convicts were they could still be con-sidered a part of 'the people', whereas intellectuals had lost all right to be considered human.

Older intellectuals, who had survived from the Old Society, had some doubts about this. But after they had been through thought reform they too accepted this kind of class analysis. As a result, very few intellectuals dared to act like criminal convicts, to pretend to be dead dogs, lie down and refuse to work.

Moving to the Main Camp meant an internal adjust-ment at the labour reform camp. Excited, the convicts discussed what changes this might mean. Their greatest concern, of course, was whether or not there might be some improvement in their own lives. The Main Camp was held to be the capital of the labour reform camp – surely it had to be better in terms of what there was to eat.

Each person carried his luggage on his back. It was fortunate that the convicts' remaining luggage was so light. There was an interesting phenomenon to be observed in this: convicts who had the most luggage turned out to be those whose bodies had not yet completely deteriorated. The weakest ones carried a pitifully small bundle of bedding. The ratio was fitting. Their pathetic belongings were all the property that these most emaciated convicts had as 'leftovers after eating'. Convicts whose bodies were still all right were either high-class convicts or men who had not yet begun to trade for food.

I had traded off a leather suitcase but I still had one left. In it, I packed my few clothes. To my eyes, these things were edibles, nothing more. They had the power to extend my life. The last act of being looked after that I enjoyed was when the Troop Leader let me throw my suitcase on to the truck that accompanied us – I could walk empty-handed.

It wasn't really very far to the Main Camp. You could see its low earthen buildings from Station Four.

21 July
Thinned sweet potatoes on Farm Eleven.
22 July
Rained, rested, got together Bai material in the morning.
Afternoon rubbed hemp rope, evening report by Division
Leader Hou.
23 July
Cut grass by farm Canal Three. Evening report by Cadre Li.
24 July
Farm Eleven thinned sweet potatoes.
25 July
Farm Eleven thinned sweet potatoes, thought about 'Aerial
Pesticide-Spraying'. Evening listened to current events
report.
26 July
Farm Eleven thinned sweet potatoes. Evening listened to
mobilization report by Camp Leader Bai. Struggled against
Wei Mingxue, I exposed a few facts.
27 July
Farm Eleven thinned sweet potatoes. Evening ceremony big
meeting, celebrating grass-pulling work productivity.
28 July
Farm Eleven thinned sweet potatoes. Fang, Li, others
recommended punishing me. Evening small-group meeting
discussed how to raise work efficiency. Finished going over
draft of 'Aerial Pesticide-Spraying'. Cut hair.
29 July
Farm Eleven thinned sweet potatoes. 'Aerial Pesticide-
Spraying' mailed to *Ningxia News*. Morning Heh Cheng
wrote a report requesting that I be punished and asked
everyone to sign. Evening cucumbers, two jin for every man.

Moving to the Main Camp meant there was a flurry of activity. First was the allocation of bunks. The Troop Leader had already marked out whose small group would be assigned to which barracks. But the right to decide who slept in which bunk belonged to that small group's leader.

Each Group Leader would arrange for those convicts he was most friendly with to be near him. The conventional wisdom was, 'At home sleep next to your woman, away from home sleep next to the wall.' The best bunks were those up against the wall. Unpopular convicts were told, 'You go under the window. Sleep by the door.'

There was in fact a certain degree of democracy inside a small group. If a rebellious convict didn't get the place he wanted, he would curse the Group Leader. If the Group Leader made him sleep by the door, this cursing would get so bad it would make the cursed ancestors of the man sleep uneasily down below. So first a Group Leader would allocate space to those who got along with him. The next ones he took care of were these bad eggs, these scum who protested. By the time he got to me, I was the one who had to sleep under the window or by the door.

None the less, I was content with my lot. When I first arrived in the camp, seven hundred days earlier, the sleeping space for each man measured only thirty centimetres wide. There was no measuring stick in the labour reform camp – we measured the thirty centimetres with a fist. A fist counted for ten centimetres: every man got three fists.

That very first day, the Group Leader's fist rolled

around on the ground, and in no time at all marked out eighteen or nineteen bunks. How was a body to get any rest on a three-fist-wide area? In fact one did learn to sleep, and indeed we slept very sweetly. Probing the universe for more living space is one of mankind's unnecessary luxuries.

By now, in 1960, the conditions of the labour reform camp had permitted expansion. I was allowed to sleep on fifty centimetres, that is on a space of five fists. I was content.

The diary entries for these days seem contradictory. On the one hand I was given responsibility by the Group Leader to organize 'material' on someone. In the struggle session I even 'exposed a few facts'. Yet various people demanded that I be punished, including Group Leader Heh Cheng. At the same time, I was still managing to write poetry in whatever nooks and crannies I could find – one can imagine what they were like. Without the genius of a Li Bai,* which I lack, how was this possible?

Best to relate the facts. As soon as we arrived at the Main Camp I followed the small group out to work. On the fifth day of thinning beets, that is, on the 26th, the Troop Leader, workmaster for the day, suddenly 'ordered me off my horse'. He let me know in no uncertain terms that I was not, as I had imagined, a high-class convict being looked after.

Thinning beets was one of the measures involved in 'crop management'. As beet plants are growing, they have to be thinned at the proper time – the straggly ones have to be plucked out, along with weeds and any shoots with bugs on them, in order to keep enough space

*Tang-dynasty poet.

between shoots and give them room to grow. Seedlings need sufficient ground area to get the nutrition to grow into strong plants. Troop Leaders generally assumed that all convicts were born to farmwork, that they instinctively knew how to do these things. If you didn't, then you were incompetent and not qualified to be a human being, let alone a convict.

In this regard, the Old Commissar was a cut above your normal Troop Leader.

One Troop Leader or another was responsible for taking a large troop to where it was to work every day. He would assign each small group to a different field, then find a place to stretch out under a shady tree. After he had rested for a while, he would occasionally make a tour of inspection. On this particular day, a Troop Leader happened to be inspecting right near me.

'Agh! What kind of thinning is this?!'

Not understanding what he meant, I raised my head to look at him. He loomed over me like a huge iron pagoda.

'You dogshitter! Sabotaging, are you?!'

The cold insinuation penetrated my bones. My whole body began to shake. One mention of sabotage and you had not made a mechanical error but a political one. I still did not understand what mistake I had made.

'Look, you!' He bent over and grabbed the beet sprouts beside me that I had thinned out. 'Agh! Everyone come look at the sprouts this dogshitter has pulled up! This is called thinning beets? He's pulled out all my best plants!'

By now we have probably all grown accustomed to this practice, from this piddling example in a labour reform camp to the large-scale corruption in China. Senior and junior managers of every organization in the country consider any property of the unit under them to be 'mine'. It is only in this one respect, of course, that they exhibit any pride of ownership. I looked at 'his' sprouts, getting ever more alarmed.

Other convicts gathered around and began to ridicule me, taking advantage of this opportunity to knock off work, get a temporary reprieve.

'Troop Leader, what he's done is pull out all the best plants!'

'It's clearly intentional sabotage!'

'No way he couldn't tell the difference between good ones and bad ones!'

'He's still an intellectual! Dogshitter.'

'He pulled out the best ones on purpose so he could eat them!' . . .

Only then did I understand. It was indeed my mistake. I was fundamentally ignorant of the purpose of thinning out the plants. On the first day of thinning, which was the first time I had ever done this work, I heard that the plants we thinned out would be sent to the kitchen and made into a vegetable dish for us. So I thought that it would be best to pluck out the juiciest, most edible sprouts. I did exactly the opposite of what was required: I did indeed intentionally pull out all the good plants. In the past few days other convicts and the Group Leader had noticed, but they hadn't warned me. So long as the Troop Leader didn't see it, the problem had nothing to do with them.

'Stand up! Dogshitter! What are you doing sitting there!' The Troop Leader was no longer frosty, he had suddenly exploded in anger. 'Quick! Get together those sprouts you've pulled up! Hang them around your neck!'

Thinning is done by sitting on the ground. It's an

easier job than hauling dirt clods. Like picking through greens, it is appropriate for those of us who were weak or in the infirmary. I never imagined that doing this easiest of jobs would bring on the greatest misfortune. Trembling all over, I crawled to my feet. With a practised hand, the Troop Leader bound the shoots I handed him with a rope he always carried. (A rope was something that a Troop Leader could not do without when he came to the fields.) He tied them into a circle, then clapped them over my dog's neck. The necklace resembled those things worn by people in the South Sea islands. The work was easy, and I had been relatively happy that day (hadn't I been writing poetry?), so I had pulled out a large number of beets, at least forty or fifty jin worth. This forty-to-fifty-jin necklace was heavy enough to force my back to bend, so that the little beets all dangled before me.

The Troop Leader still had a length of rope left, which was just the right size to make a leash to pull me along by.

'Move! Dogshitter! Follow me!'

Practically crawling behind him, I followed his rear end. I didn't know, wasn't concerned about, didn't even care where he was taking me. He didn't in fact take me anywhere – just had me follow him around the beet fields like a dog. As we moved along, he swore at me and my crime.

'Agh! Look, everyone! I want everyone to look here! This dogshitter, you know how he's been sabotaging? He didn't thin out the bad shoots, he very carefully pulled up all the good ones! What do you think? How about a struggle session against this dogshitter!'

This was the procedure known as being photographed.

This specific kind was only one among hundreds of strange poses.

Over one hundred convicts were thinning beets just then in over one hundred mou of beet fields. This was an unexpected chance for them to have some fun. I couldn't see the look in their eyes, but I could hear their sneering. Row after row of beet plants streamed by as we walked around and around, seemingly for ever. My tears and the snot from my nose flowed together; the yellow and green glistened on my chin.

In explanation, it should be pointed out here that China has had a tradition for thousands of years to the effect that a gentleman, a superior man, can be killed but he can't be scorned. This tradition ended abruptly in 1957. From that date our leaders, for the first time in history, made the ridiculing of a man's character a means of education. Senior intellectuals, docile and obedient, agreed with them. In countless criticism-and-struggle sessions all over the country, they acquiesced and appeared to adopt the attitude that they should demean themselves by helping their criticizers. With these elders, these superiors, serving as an example, how could you blame others? How could you blame the malnourished young green leaf that I was for thinking that the Troop Leader's punishment was really a form of education? Even though I felt that this particular form was some-what severe.

The ugly swearing of the Troop Leader was a means of expressing his anger at seeing the country's property destroyed; the ridicule of the convicts was a means of expressing their contempt for a person who hadn't the most basic understanding of farming. That is the only way I could comprehend it. It could not really be called 'comprehension', though, for right then I was unable to use my brain for any rational analysis. I had given myself over to the laws of inertia. Without shame and without anger, truly like a dog or a donkey, I obediently followed the Troop Leader around in a circle.

After this, the most sympathetic words spoken to me were, 'Don't think the Troop Leader *wants* to punish you. He really has your own interests in mind.' After hearing a lot of this kind of thing later, I learned to give similar comfort to others.

After having me circle the fields with a necklace of beets around my neck, the Troop Leader luckily did not also order that my rations be cut. In the past seven hundred and some days, I had seen many poor bastards get both the photograph punishment and reduced rations.

At noon, the mess cart brought thin grass soup to the beet fields. The convicts split into their groups and lined up to get their food. Cowed and dejected, I too joined the food line, all the while keeping a secret watch on the Troop Leader seated in the shade of a tree. As though nothing had happened, he was already lifting the cover off his lunchbox and mixing together the rice and vegetables inside, as though he hadn't just exploded in anger, as though I had never done anything wrong. When I too had my quota of lunch safely in hand, not a bit less than it should have been, I even felt ever so slightly grateful to the Troop Leader.

The written word has given mankind plenty of headaches ever since we invented it. By the time history had developed up to the middle part of the twentieth century, the practice of 'rectifying documentary material' had begun. The labour camps were no exception. Bai's case, mentioned in the diary entry on 22 July, was only one among thousands and tens of thousands of cases in the camps, and the documentary material of each of these cases had to be rectified. The number of cases in the entire country is astronomical. It is incalculable. Any individual was qualified to rectify anybody else's material – no legal body had to be concerned or involved. And the moment an event was set on paper, fixed into words, no matter how brief and unimportant it might have been, it was established for ever, as though nailed down with an iron plate over it.

China has long had a saying, 'When a word goes through the public gate, nine oxen can't haul it out again.' The written word is revered in China, perhaps because of the number of illiterate people. But as a result, no other language in the world has the same ability as Chinese to skewer people and time, to pin them down. The mutual rectification of documents created enemies among people, which was probably exactly what the leaders wanted.

Bai was no more than a petty thief. After coming into the camps, his stealing naturally became much worse. The material that I was given the honour of rectifying was nothing more than a record of his various thieving accomplishments: several stems of vegetables, several carrots, edibles that had been sent by somebody else's family, etc. The list was given to me by his small group, which had in turn collected the data from the whole body of convicts. When sufficient material had been accumulated, he would be punished.

My pulling out good beet sprouts instead of bad ones was qualitatively a different kind of mistake from that of Bai. Bai's mistake, stealing after he had come into the camp, was still an internal contradiction among the people. My mistake was regarded as a contradiction between the people and the enemy. Since my act had been so 'destructive', the contradiction was even sharper. And so, 'Fang, Li, others recommended punishing me,' 'Heh Cheng wrote a report requesting that I be punished and asked everyone to sign.' This was all quite understandable.

Chinese democracy manifests itself in mutual surveillance. It also shows itself in the fact that whenever anyone is to be praised or punished the decision has to go through a process of group deliberation. The labour reform camps were the same as everywhere else. There are only a couple of names recorded in the diary, but it is certain that the entire group of convicts agreed unanimously that I should be punished. The mass-deliberation process had taken place. The next step was to see what arrangements the leaders would make.

Poets have their weaknesses but they also have a tough side. When they find themselves in adverse conditions, it spurs on their ability to survive. If there is nothing else to rely on, they can get through by chanting poetry. The hand might be too weak to wring a chicken's neck, but it is still strong enough to wield a pen. And so while this mass-deliberation process was deciding to punish me, I was even more actively writing poetry.

The title of my poem, 'Aerial Pesticide-Spraying', lacked some of the poetic feeling of 'Shine on, Crimson Rays'. But, as Goethe once noted, there is nothing in the world that cannot be written into poetry. Wasn't an aeroplane poetic, flying over the magnificent countryside as it sprayed chemicals? I knew perfectly well that I would not be able to mail this poem out, and that even if I could it had a miniscule chance of getting published. My purpose was not to see my words in a journal, but to hope that the leaders in the camps who inspected letters would read in them my political sincerity, as well as my literary talent. I was lousy at hard labour, but I had other abilities to supplement my deficiencies. If this worked, the camp authorities might place me among the ranks of high-class convicts – and preserve my life.

'You must give a good impression of yourself.'

'Your performance has to get better.'

'What's your impression of your own behaviour lately? You should do a thorough evaluation of yourself . . .'

These phrases had not only become colloquialisms among the leaders as they criticized or admonished intellectuals, they were also seen in all the editorials in newspapers. With the passage of time, 'a good performance', or 'a good manifestation of oneself', became a standard of behaviour for intellectuals.

Intellectuals used all kinds of 'intellect', irrespective of what form it took, to try to 'manifest' their political attitude. Exposing other people, raising questions about others and investigating them, vigorously participating in criticism-and-struggle sessions, even drawing a clear line between themselves and parents who had raised them with great love but whose class standing was bad – these were all methods of expressing oneself, or performing well.

Couldn't the writing of poetry and prose also be considered a kind of high-brow means of political expression? If one agreed that literature was an art-form through which mankind expressed itself, then this form

98

now had a new meaning, a new responsibility. Literary arts can flourish in any kind of social environment.

Writing poetry and prose to express oneself was not always direct enough, however. After them came a more direct form of expression. As the next entry in the diary puts it, 'Struggled against Wei Mingxue, I exposed a few facts.'

Wei was a criminal convict – he appears again later in this diary. Intellectuals who consider themselves to be lofty and pure generally do not condescend to 'expose facts'. Who among these lofty men has been denounced, though, just after they have plucked out all the good beets? It is hard to attend to high ideals when one is pressed to the wall. When an entire stratum of intellectuals in China was pressed to the wall, it can be said with confidence that every one of those intellectuals informed on others. They all, at the very least, exposed a few facts during criticism-and-struggle sessions.

It was like syphilis: when syphilis became widespread, it ceased to be such a disgraceful disease, to the point that it even became a kind of badge of honour. It showed you'd been out whoring.

During these last nine days, 21–29 July, there were six notations about listening to reports. I used the word 'report'. But what did the leaders of labour reform camps feel obliged to report to convicts? They did not have to report to us on plans, or on their successful implementation, but rightists and other political prisoners still insisted on calling the haranguing and the verbal abuse 'reports'.

'Report time!'

'Hurry up, everyone together to hear the Commissar's report!'

'X X-x, you're too xxxxxxx slow! Report's about to begin!'

The whistle would scream through the camp almost every night, together with this kind of shouting.

These reports were actually no more than an excuse to abuse us. They were mainly composed of strings of violent cursing. Thinking back on it, the mental suffering that intellectuals went through at this time was the result of their own over-developed sensitivity. Throughout the long course of history, we have never played our preordained role very well. When we were to be convicts, we couldn't quite get the part right. When we were to be enemies, we found them impossible to play. We were always madly trying to embrace the other side, even though we were told we should be against it. Even the terminology, the concepts we used, were indistinguishable from those of our adversaries. Whatever term they devised we automatically adopted. We were not afraid of their pushing us into the depths of material scarcity, but we were unbearably hurt by their telling us that our thinking was not the same as theirs.

Off we would go for the reports. Mid-summer was when the mosquitoes were at their height, and when the sun had gone behind the mountains they would bite most fiercely. One could still swat at them while working in the fields, but the Troop Leaders absolutely forbade convicts to move their arms or legs while listening to a report. We were forced to stand to attention. Still, we convicts had our convict ways: we sewed a kind of hood out of rags, which we put over our heads. We looked something like America's KKK.

Naturally, the Troop Leader didn't like this, and yelled at us for being Little Capitalist Gentlemen. 'If a couple of mosquito bites get to you, what are you going to do when the enemy grabs you? When they take you up for torture you'll blurt it all out! Right?'

This kind of analogy made us feel like underground revolutionary workers. It seemed that even the Troop Leaders couldn't agree on our proper role.

Mosquitoes hummed around men who were exhausted; added to this were tirades that were not exactly stimulating. None the less, before 1959 people could still force themselves to take it. After the policy changed to one of lowered-rations-to-be-substituted-with-gourds-and-greens, though, convicts would simply faint and fall over. We were like dominoes: when one started, everyone would go. The threshing ground would be covered with fallen bodies. Among them, of course, were pretenders. These were criminal convicts. Most of the intellectuals would do their utmost to 'continue to be educated' until they died from the effort.

Finally, after the Old Commissar gave special permission, everyone was allowed to sit on the ground if reports went on too long.

Mind you, we still had reports. The Old Commissar told the Troop Leaders: 'You can't let them have free time in the evenings! If there's nothing to do after work, then give them more reports. These scoundrels will think up nasty tricks if you leave them to their own devices. If they can't sit up, they'll have to listen lying down!

'If there really isn't anything to report, then read to them from the newspaper. Read until it's time for them to go to sleep.'

30 July
Cut hemp on Farm Sixteen! 'Entertainment evening'. Divvied up tobacco, one pack per six people (seven fen).*
31 July
Rest – uninteresting day. Depressed. Farm Sixteen cut hemp. Double-Counter mobilization meeting in the evening. Troop Leader song, Division Leader Zhang reported.
2 August
Farm Sixteen cut hemp. Got letter from *Ningxia News*. Said 'Forever' manuscript did not accord with reality, not planning to publish it. Informing on and exposing others for Double-Counter Movement – every man must write two of them.
3 August
Farm Sixteen cut hemp. Listened to Old Commissar's report in the evening, talked about problems of reforming ourselves.
4 August
Farm Sixteen cut hemp. Bought six jiao worth of tobacco, 1 jiao 4 fen of salt.
5 August
Farm Sixteen cut hemp. Listened to Old Commissar's report in the evening, talked about problems of production. Wrote a big-character poster on Su Xiaosu.

*Chinese money is divided into yuan, jiao and fen, similar to the pound, shilling and penny of Britain.

*F*rom reading this diary, it might seem as though a convict's life was traumatic but also rich in colour. In addition to hard labour, there were reports to listen to, small-group meetings to attend, democratic surveillance, mutual exposing, vigorous informing. There were requests for people to sign petitions to punish others, there were victory meetings, struggle sessions. On one particular day, indeed, there was an evening of entertainment.

Several years later, I happened to meet a released convict from 'labour-reform-and-labour-education' who had been a middle-school teacher. We sat together at a small food stall at the end of a street, and began to talk about this most interesting slice of life that we had both experienced.

'Do you know why I was always treated as a high-class convict when I was in labour reform?' he asked me.

I said I didn't know why. He drew me back to the memory of that mid-summer evening of entertainment in 1960.

No matter how primitive the conditions, in addition to rousing the convicts with reports, the labour camps would hold plays, put on movies and so on. Though the convicts would rather have gone home to sleep than accept the leaders' kindness in offering them these things to do, attendance at such entertainment was mandatory. It was one more means of education. Unless a man was close to dying, he had to get down to the threshing ground to 'enjoy' it.

Some convicts thought that reports could not be

missed, but that movies and plays were different. They tried to grab the chance to get some rest on their kangs. This was a mistake – these people were severely beaten. 'You try to do them a favour, and they don't even know how to accept it!' the Old Commissar would yell. 'Motherfuckers! You put on a play for them and they don't even go to watch. Now you listen to me, and listen carefully! You'll watch this play, and I'm warning you – after watching there'll be discussion!'

Often it would be hard to see the social significance in the musical or skit, to figure out just how this theatre was useful in your thought reform. As a result, this kind of entertainment left a shroud of gloom hanging over us.

There was no itinerant troop of actors who came around to perform for us. It was now that the convicts I mentioned earlier, who could act, sing or dance, were needed. Two or three days before a performance, these people would be let off work to practise. The plays were mostly local productions, such as 'The Poor Man's Hatred of the Rich', 'Blood-&-Tears Enemy', etc. The themes reflected the class struggle of the Old Society. If a convict was sent into the camps who had a speciality, such as acrobatics or singing, then we would get to see something new. But the cadres of the camps seemed to like local plays in particular, and they were extremely well versed in them. As the convicts performed up on stage, they would nod their heads in time to the music, fingers tapping legs, as though they were mesmerized.

They were the only ones who could muster the energy to show real appreciation. Whichever convict performed the best was sure to be taken care of by his Troop Leader. One local star, a man from the neighbouring area, was consistently taken care of – he was treated as a high-class convict until his release. Still, it is hard to sing well on an empty stomach. Even Mei Lanfang* himself would have found it hard to keep up standards. And so, except for that one local star, there weren't many convicts who enjoyed this favourable treatment.

Entertainment evenings were mostly thrown together on the spur of the moment. When the performance was over, the stage would be taken down and each performer would return to his own group to work in the big fields again. By the end of 1960, after every description of man had been swept up into the labour-reform-camp net, the Labour Reform Bureau of the area finally set up a more substantial, official theatre troop. It was called the Reborn Theatre Troop. At first, this troop performed only for the labour reform state farms. Later it developed into a travelling tour and went to various cities and counties. Audiences received this group much more favourably than the professional theatres. Since many famous actors and actresses had become convicts, they could now be seen only in the Reborn Theatre Troop. But this is a story for some other time.

In August 1960, the Reborn Theatre Troop was still an ad hoc group. Its makeshift stage was built in front of the threshing ground. On either side of the stage were two gas lamps, so bright they hurt everyone's eyes. Black-clothed convicts sat like a flock of crows on the dark wintry ground of the threshing floor. As usual, the crazy sound of coughing came first: it was the pro-logue to any show. A tent was erected towards the back of the threshing ground to serve as dressing rooms; it

*A famous Peking opera star.

was lit with candles so that the actors could put on their make-up.

The middle-school teacher related how that day he was playing a bit part, called a running-dragon part. He was also responsible for helping out the actors. After a while, a camp leader we all knew pulled aside the curtain to the dressing rooms and stomped inside. He looked around, then said, 'These candles are useless. They're not bright enough. You there!' he called to a female convict who was an actress, 'come along with me to the Main Camp office, help me get some better ones.'

As this teacher mentioned her, I recalled that actress: she truly was a superior specimen among the convicts. In fact, she is still a major actress in China today. She had a very slender figure, two long black braids and a pair of big glistening eyes. The middle-school teacher said that after the two of them had been gone for a long time, it was getting to be her time to be on stage. The Troop Leader told him to go and find the actress on the double and bring her back.

Obeying the command, he left. He found the office. It was pitch-dark inside – not a light was on. He said he had already begun to have a premonition, anticipating that this man and woman might be up to a little something. So he crawled up to the window and looked inside, all the while coughing as loudly as he could. This provoked a response: the camp leader flung open the door and stridently bellowed. 'Wha'dya want?!'

'Camp leader, please have X X-x hurry up and get on stage!' he said, allowing a certain prickly tone into his voice. Having announced this, he turned and fled.

'The next day,' he continued, 'I wrote an accusation to the Labour Reform Bureau, reporting that the camp leader was messing with female convicts. Not many days later, the camp leader transferred me to guard the root cellar. As you know yourself, this job was even better than being a cadre. You just sat there without moving, without having to say a word. If you wanted something to eat – you had it right there. Except for the Old Commissar, I could be considered the luckiest man in the camp.

'Later, the minute some movement appeared on the horizon, such as the Double-Counter Movement or the Point-out-and-Attack Movement, when things got a bit tense, in other words, all I had to do was write a little accusation to the superiors. I would intentionally let the censors find my letter and hand it over to the camp leader.

'The trick was truly effective: I was never touched by any informing or exposing. I was never struggled against or criticized. In the morning I would sleep as long as I liked before getting up. Cadres would ask me and I'd say I had worked all night; in the evening as soon as the sky darkened I'd lie down on the kang – cadres would try to make trouble but I'd tell them I had worked all day. Sometimes, when the camp leader ran into me, he would snicker and say, "You're doing great! Keep up the good work." The pigs would grunt around there in the pantry, dogs would come scavenging, and I wouldn't even kick them out. I stayed fat and fair-skinned till the time I got out.'

By the time I was hearing this story, both of us were classified as 'released-convicts-from-labour-reform-and-labour-education'. The daily circumstances of his existence were now worse than when he was a proper labour reform convict. He sighed as he said, 'I feel a little nostalgic for those times.'

His reporting and my writing poetry and prose were tricks that played a different tune but had the same function. But somehow, accusations seemed to be more persuasive than poetry to the leaders.

After the female convict was released, she too became a released-convict-from-labour-reform-and-labour-education. When she went back to her home town, she couldn't find any work, so the only thing to do was go back to the labour reform camp, hoping that the farm would take her in as an agricultural worker. The work done by released convicts working in a labour reform state farm was much easier than the work they would have had to do out in society. Not only could they avoid the normal pressures of the outside world, but they held a higher status than the normal convicts around them. The camp leader said a word or two and she was allowed back in.

Later she married a worker on the farm and had a child. When I was made a convict a second time and put back into labour in this particular camp, her child was already walking. Working in the fields, people would occasionally see the mother. She had a spring in her step, and seemed happy – her body had filled out and her face was content. Using the middle-school teacher's words, she had grown fat and fair-skinned. The camp leader was still there, still the head of the place, just a little older. I examined his features and thought that he looked a little more mellow. If he had wanted to take revenge on the middle-school teacher who had accused him it would have been as easy as turning over his hand. He would simply have had him rectified to death. I've seen too many similar cases. Someone in authority does a shameless deed and then turns around and blames a convict.

As a result, I couldn't help but feel a bit of respect for this dissolute camp leader who managed to stay human and keep up old friendships.

The middle-school teacher and I parted ways on the street, but that summer evening in 1960 went round and round in my head. You may note that there was a kind of code in the diary: I cut hemp from 30 July to 5 August, but only on the 30th of July did I write an exclamation mark after the entry. This punctuation was imbued with gratitude. After that was 'Rest – uninteresting day.' It was extremely difficult to gain any rest in the labour camps: how could I find it 'uninteresting'?

'Farm Sixteen' meant the sixteenth canal of the main farm of the labour reform camp. The fields of the camp were divided up and numbered according to the canals that ran through them. The many branches that came off the great canal were called branch canals; the water of these branch canals flowed on down into farm canals and passed through the various farms, irrigating the fields. Farm Sixteen was the sixteenth farm canal coming off a branch canal, and it was where we cut hemp. This particular kind of hemp, called *buma*, is also known as *yama*. The hemp grown in the north-west was mainly *yama*, which is used for oil.

Harvesting crops in mid-summer meant working in fields that burned your feet, they were scorched so hot by the sun. It was a hard job that made you sweat as though it was raining. The lucky thing was that tonight would be entertainment – meaning we could knock off work early. I had originally planned to throw my thin, exhausted body on to my 'home' for a minute, let it stretch out flat and give it a breather, but the Troop Leader ordered the Group Leader to tell me to go to Headquarters.

When I got there, a Troop Leader I didn't recognize asked me my name and, after confirming who I was, told me to report to the place where the actors were rehearsing. Although I had been unsuccessful in getting any rest, this was positive news: were they intending to take care of me again? A little more cheerful, I made my way to the rehearsal room.

This room, made of dirt clods, was especially high-ceilinged and large. It was an empty granary, and the air still carried the musty odour of grain. The actors inside were rehearsing boisterously. One old convict in tattered prison rags was putting on the airs of a landlord. He pulled on a fake tuft of beard below his chin and stuck out a pitifully small, bony chest as he walked grandly back and forth. Like an itinerant entertainer with his trained monkeys, the Troop Leader in charge of the performance sat up high on a window ledge giving instructions. Seeing me, he jumped down and said:

'I called you over here because you can write words.' Writing poetry or prose was all the same to the Troop Leaders: in their eyes, it was all 'writing words'. 'Take these two songbooks away and make me two copies. Quick, because we'll need them right away!'

I asked him where I should make the copies. Should I take them back to the barracks?

He thought that over, and finally said, 'No, don't go back. Just do it here – I'll find you some room. It'll be faster that way.'

He led me to a small room next door where hemp

110

bags, ropes and other odds and ends were kept. There he stuffed a pen and paper into my hands. 'Be quick! And you're not allowed to make mistakes. Plus you'd better write the words beautifully. This is for the uppers to inspect before we use it.'

After he left, I looked over the libretto. Amazed, I couldn't help but wonder why anyone should go to the trouble of inspecting it. The songs had long since been published by national publishing houses; they had been performed tens of thousands of times. Luckily, the job was easy. Songs and poetry alike are divided into lines – even an 'Ah!' got its own line. It looked like a lot, but when it came to copying the book it was easy. There was also carbon paper, so that making two copies meant I only had to write it once.

I squatted down beside a large scale sitting on the floor, and wrote on its weighing platform. With a stiff piece of paper underneath to support my work, I quickly copied out the slim songbook as the Troop Leader had ordered. After that, I still had free time. Unwilling to leave with empty hands, I looked around to see if there weren't a little something in this grain storage room that I could eat. Just as I was looking around, turning over various things to see if there might be something under them, a convict-actress walked in.

'Troop Leader told me to come see how far you'd written.'

I said I had copied it all.

'Oh! Well, you're pretty fast!' She picked up the songs from the scale and flipped through them one by one, singing some of the words as she turned the pages. ' "You vampire! You evil man-eating spirit – you blood sucker! Today I'm going to clear up all your old debts . . .'"

Uneasily, I stood beside the scales secretly watching her, afraid that she might have noticed me turning things over. What are you looking for? Thinking of stealing something, are you? But, after observing her for a moment, I had the feeling that she was different from myself and the other male convicts. Women and men may wear the same clothes, but the clothes exaggerate the special attributes of a woman's body. While all of us male convicts had caved-in, emaciated chests, this woman was endowed with two small mounds of flesh. I was amazed.

Really quite plump! I said to myself with envy. Her face was lively, even exuberant, her short hair was jet black and gleaming. In the golden light of evening, her soft, slender neck shone like jade, quite unlike the necks of us male convicts – all skin and sinews, like chicken necks that have had their feathers plucked out. Accustomed to seeing death masks, I was perplexed: could she possibly be eating as much as she wanted?

'Yes! It's written quite well,' she complimented me as she organized the stack of papers and gave it a little pat. Still she did not leave. Her eyes lingered on my face, as she asked, 'Is your name X X-x?'

I said it was. But as I did, I wondered, Is she going to inform on me? Could she be making sure of the name so she could go back and write a little report? At the last entertainment evening they had played an extremely 'red' opera, first shown at the revolutionary base of Yan'an, called *Brothers and Sisters, Open up the Frontier*. The brother played a joke on the sister by pretending to be asleep when the government was assigning work.

The sister came and saw this, and sang out to the audience, 'I'm going to report this to Division Commander Liu, and tomorrow we'll hold a meeting and have you struggled against!' If a little sister could report on an older brother, why couldn't a female convict report on someone who was a complete stranger?

The look in her eyes suddenly softened, as she put her hand very gently on my shoulder. She impulsively brushed her face up close to mine. In that brief moment, the only thing I saw was her tongue. A good half of it was protruding from her lips, and I noticed that the end was pink.

With a flying leap, I shook off her hand and ran from the room. Normally, I would never have been able to accomplish such a quick reaction.

My heart was still pounding when I got back to the barracks. I had no idea what she had stuck her tongue out for – what she meant to do with it. It was the strangest thing I had ever seen in the twenty-three years of my life. Certainly less comprehensible than the fact that, as soon as I could, I had begun turning things over in that granary to try to find something to eat.

When the performance began that evening, she was up there on stage, singing away. In fact, she seemed to be the main character in this local play, playing the role of a young girl oppressed by a landlord. In the end the young woman joins the revolution and returns to her home town to help liberate the poor. Her acting was quite normal, and from the expressions of the Troop Leaders, who actively enjoyed it, clearly her singing was considered passable. How could she suddenly go so crazy?

Throughout the next day, a day of 'rest', I thought

over this extraordinary experience. Gradually, unconsciously, I became aware that she had not in fact had bad intentions. I had sensed an unusual gentleness and warmth when her hand was placed on my shoulder. But just at that moment I was in mortal fear of being found out and exposed. Now that the danger had passed, I was more and more convinced that her intentions were good ones. As a result, I began to regret losing such a chance. If she were indeed good-hearted, I could have invited her to go through the room together with me, to see if any of the grain that had once been there was left.

I now remembered that in the moment when she pushed the door open and walked in, I seemed to have noticed a bulging hemp bag off to one side. It was strictly forbidden to store pesticides in the granary. If that bag wasn't edible rice, or wheat, or some other grain, then what could it have been? As a convict, as a person with an extremely emaciated body, someone whose hands and feet could hardly move, not only had I been in a place that was perhaps piled high with food, but I had been in possession of a brief moment of liberty – and yet I had let the opportunity go.

As a result, I was unhappy during the entire next day of resting. I felt depressed. I watched the other convicts going in and out, trading things, cooking up radishes and cabbage, eating soup and the dry flatbread that families had sent from home, and I thought, If only yesterday I could have interpreted her intentions in a better light. If I could have seized the moment and opened those hemp bags with her, then I might be sitting here on the kang today gnawing as hard as I could!

The Shakespeares, Tolstoys, Li Bais, Du Fus and Cao Xuejins who had nurtured me had never mentioned the

114

utility of a tongue in making love, other than to have it express declarations of ardour. Plays, movies, even those 1940s movies from Hollywood, had never shown a tongue in action so that I could understand its function. Kissing was, after all, a matter of lips. I had seen that in movies and read plenty about it in books. Perhaps I had seen it too much. The concept of love in my mind had become fixed, established, so that it excluded taking any other form. When I personally encountered a different form, I thought it unnatural. I was unnerved by it and fled.

Many years later, when a woman expertly thrust her tongue into my mouth for the first time, I was not aroused. Instead my thoughts returned to that incident of so many years before. A spectre suddenly appeared before me, and at last I knew what this young actress was trying to express, what the extended pink tip of her tongue had meant.

The woman was sleeping beside me that night, but I had lost interest in her. Tears filled my eyes as I fiercely remembered that female convict. In the summer of 1960, when many Chinese had either died of hunger or were on the verge of dying, in a dilapidated little room that had been used for storing grain in a remote labour reform camp in the north-west, she had played out a scene that was both beautiful and terribly human. The pink tip of her tongue now turned into a true red flag, beckoning me not to a Communist paradise but to a true paradise on earth. She had been so brave, so liberated, supernaturally un-vulgar, completely oblivious to the false, defeated, tragic world around her, that it shocked me into understanding. Her actions revealed another, natural, world to me.

I not only don't know her name, I have even forgotten her face. The passage of time, none the less, has brought the fact of her into ever sharper focus. Her face and body seem perfect to me, and the vibrations, the aura she gave off, have defined 'feminine' for me ever since. Actions that I could not understand at the time have now become classic and elegant in my mind. She has already become a song that lingers when I am lonely, that tells me to believe in people. They may be trying to 'express themselves', to 'put in a performance' in the political sense, but their true selves are stubbornly holding on. Later, when I was being struggled against, when I was being criticized, I did not feel antipathy towards those who criticized, for I believed that there was also a true self within them.

My middle-school-teacher friend said he longed for the days when he was sent to guard the root cellar by the camp leader. After his luck turned, however, and he was able to eat his fill, I dare say he forgot about the earlier days. In contrast, the strange experience I had, that brief moment of miraculous fortune, is something that I will remember for ever.

I was lucky. Although it lasted for two seconds at the most, those two seconds have blessed my entire life.

In the summer of 1960, even starving, even in extremity, how was it with a man and a woman? How could it be? Well?!

6–8 August
Farm Fifteen planted vegetables with the Vegetable Group.
9 August
Cut grass on Farm Three branch canal along with the Main
Work Troop.
10 August
Rained. Study session in morning. Groups 17 and 18 held
meeting to struggle against Zhu Zhenbang, I recorded.
Afternoon Main Work Troop went out to work, I stayed home
to rub grass into rope.
11 August
Went with Main Work Troop to work at Farm Three branch
canal; I cut grass. Small-group discussion meeting in the
evening.
12 August
Held rewards-and-punishments meeting for second half 1960.
Ten people arrested, thirteen people graduated. Received
three-yuan remittance from mother.

*T*his romantic episode passed like a spark. I was oblivious of how beautiful it had been, and so did not have any feeling of being sorry for myself. Afterwards, I didn't ask anyone for her name, and, except to be depressed, I obviously didn't think much about it. If I could be called disappointed, it was only on behalf of that bulging hemp bag. Nothing more.

Several days after moving to the Main Camp, I was being looked after again. From the entries in the diary, it is clear that I skipped going to work with the Main Work Troop for several days. Instead, I went first with the Vegetable Group to plant vegetables. After that, even though I accompanied another small group to the rice paddies, while others plunged into the mud soup to pull weeds I stayed on the bank, using a broken old sickle to cut grass.

I worked as hard as I could, feeling grateful for my luck. Seeing the tribulations of others makes one appreciate one's own good fortune. For twenty-four hours a day we convicts were stuck in the middle of a pile of men. The slightest turn of the body meant rubbing up against somebody else, so that to be working alone in the dense reeds and grass was extremely satisfying. One could bury one's head and get on with cutting. There wasn't a person to be seen around me. Above was only the clean, bright blue sky and the solitary orb of the sun. Through crisp jade-green reeds a breeze stirred up sparkling ripples on the water. Seagull-like water birds spread their wings as they called overhead. Lines from a Northern Song poet named Liu Yong suddenly welled up inside me:

Waking from the wine this evening, where am I?
Willows on the banks, a breeze, a last remaining sliver
of moon.

Numbness and intoxication are not very different. Being numb can bring you to much the same place as being drunk.

There are several points regarding these particular entries that I want to make. Why, for example, they should arrest people during a rewards-and-punishments meeting. Could convicts actually be arrested, even while serving their time? Also, in the context of a labour reform camp, what was the meaning of 'graduation'?

To be accurate, we were now undergoing the 'educational nurturing of labour'. It was said at the time that this was an administrative form of punishment in accord with the principle of managing 'contradictions-between-the-people-and-their-enemies' as though they were 'internal-contradictions-among-the-people'. This meant that the government did not treat us as enemies, although we were considered to be enemies. Instead, with great generosity, the government gathered us together on farms and gave us the benefit of farming expertise so that we might remake ourselves into new people.

Our farm, however, was under the jurisdiction of the Labour Reform Leaders of the Public Security system. Other than not having military patrols to guard us, everything else was managed according to the dictates of labour reform. In name we were above the status of normal labour reform convicts but, from what we knew of their treatment, we were in constant envy of their situation.

For example, normal labour reform convicts all had fixed sentences. The sentences had been determined by a court. Even if their work did not come up to the mark, if these men didn't commit a crime again they were freed when the sentence was up. But those of us being labour-education-nurtured, on the other hand, had no fixed sentence. We would 'graduate' when we had sufficiently reformed. It sounded lovely: to graduate. But, Lord! What did it mean to be sufficiently reformed? One had to give everything, one's life-blood, to achieve it.

The most immediate, real benefit that attached to being a normal criminal convict was that these men had security guards watching over them. When the guards' work hours were over, they would lead the men back to the barracks, regardless of whether or not the work was actually finished. The convicts followed the guards quite obediently, having worked a regular eight-hour day. If it happened to be inclement weather, like howling wind with sand and grit in it, or a heavy mist restricting visibility, these convicts were allowed to stay locked up in their barracks and not go out. With labour-education-nurturing convicts, it was 'Off to work!' And only when the field work was done were we allowed to come 'home'.

Before the policy of 'lowered-rations-to-be-substituted-with-gourds-and-greens' began in 1960, we worked every day, no days off, for twelve hours a day. During the Great Leap Forward of 1958, we often worked from the time you could see your fingers in the morning until you couldn't see them at night: up to eighteen hours a day.

Although this labour-education-nurturing brought many inconveniences to us convicts, it presented a convenient opportunity for the leaders. It gave them a chance to send large numbers of people into labour reform camps. For example, if some intellectuals had said one or two things that implied mistaken thinking, or even if some had said nothing wrong at all, if any leaders had feelings against them it was 'Send them to court!'

They lacked bad enough credentials to be judged and sentenced, however. What to do?

'Send them off to be labour-education-reformed!'

The numbers just happened to match the quota for rightists that had been established by senior authorities. Seven hundred days earlier, at the time I had been thrown in, society was shipping off a large quantity of fresh blood to the labour reform camps. One day, coming back from work, I saw a country bumpkin, a peasant, squatting beside the door to our barracks and crying. How could this kind of person be classed as a rightist? When I asked him, he was sniffling so hard he couldn't answer. Later, from what others said, I figured it out. The man came from a county that was sending twenty rightists into the camp. The men who were to guard them had already been appointed, but this young man wanted badly to take advantage of an opportunity to see the outside world. So he petitioned to be allowed to go on the expedition.

He begged insistently and the leaders finally agreed. He and a cadre would go together, guarding the rightists as they went to the camp. On the way, however, one of the rightists escaped. The two men who were guarding the group made an emergency long-distance phone call back to the county to ask what to do.

'We need twenty,' said the Party leaders. 'One's gone.

Not enough to fill the required quota . . .' So they had him plug the hole with himself.

So simple! It was unnecessary to mess with any legal proceedings. At most, you had to process a form called 'change of residence'. There were not many legal hoops to jump through in any event, but it was still less trouble to jump through one than it was to jump through two. I can guarantee that this unlucky bastard who wanted to use public funds to take a sightseeing trip died in the camps. People who felt they were wronged were destined for a short life. Those who made it through were those who, as it was said, 'admitted their crimes and accepted the punishment'. Only then could one proceed with a calm mind, and focus all of one's thoughts and energies on getting enough food.

The words 'labour-education-nurturing' give a warm and friendly impression. If you had been a lazy bum, with no talent or desire to work, when you came in here you could learn a new trade – you could become a New Man who brought benefit to society. You might have committed some little crime, but instead of sentencing you as a criminal convict, they let you continue to enjoy being called one of the 'people'. All they did was take away a little of your freedom. After all, you were not being subjected to legal punishment, but rather to the highest administrative punishment. When you had sufficiently reformed, and had graduated, whatever you were supposed to do in the future you would gladly do.

During the anti-rightist movement one leader of a certain unit, who had a slightly Confucian air about him, saw various men below him being sent to the camps to be reformed. Since he had a compassionate and benign nature, he actually volunteered to go and do labour reform himself. One had to reform anyway, there on the Outside, so his logic was, why not do it properly, all the way, in a regular labour reform camp? That way, he could be even more disciplined and sincere about it.

He applied to the authorities to be allowed to receive labour-education-nurturing, and he was promptly put on one of the name-lists. This sort of gentleman was exactly the sort the authorities least liked anyway. They were happy to put him on a boat down the river.

'Fine! You want to do that – go ahead!'

He arrived, and even slept beside me for a while, on one of those thirty-centimetre-wide bed spaces. Before long, he had died. Like those who felt wronged, his type, who were too honest, would also generally die. They were incapable of protecting themselves.

'Properly and correctly managing internal contradictions *among the people*' was a common saying at that time. What it meant was that first a large group of people would be targeted as *enemies of the people*. Then the group would be told that in name they were still being treated as *part* of 'the people', even as they were put in the position of being the people's enemies.

Criminal convicts were the first to discover that in many respects labour-education-nurturing was worse than being a regular convict. They recognized that what superficially sounded like a distinction actually was no distinction at all. I've become aware that people without much culture are often able to see things more clearly than those who are educated. They are able to take the understanding into their bones, so to speak. They trust their own impressions of reality. They don't easily believe what is written in books, on paper, in documents. It isn't easy to pour high and abstruse theories of propaganda into these people's heads. In seven hundred days, I saw many criminal convicts who were with us being labour-education-nurtured intentionally elevating themselves to the ranks of regular, sentenced convicts. Especially during that period when we had to work eighteen hours a day.

'Returned-to-the-palace' convicts, who had had the good fortune to be regular convicts before, described their previous lives as though they had been romping around in heaven. These men were unafraid of violating the system. They had no fear of being criticized and struggled against. They were sublimely unconcerned about all those things that intellectual convicts were scared to death of. This diary carries a number of references to 'exposing' someone, to criticizing and struggling against someone, to writing big-character posters about someone. All those someones were criminal convicts.

One did not lightly grab on to the mistakes of an intellectual convict, except for something like my stupidly mistaking good beets for bad beets and pulling them out. Criticizing an intellectual could bring terrible retribution. As a result, every word we spoke was like a mouse: before leaving its hole, it had to poke its nose out and look carefully around. If it saw so much as a shadow, it would draw back.

The man who was being struggled against on 10 August, Zhu Zhenbang, was an unemployed vagrant who stole things from time to time. He had dared to say that the policy of 'lowered-rations-to-be-substituted-with-gourds-and-greens' was like using a wooden knife to kill a man.

This was something that intellectuals would never dare to utter. That goes without saying, but they would also not even dare to think it. It was both an extremely poisonous and extremely vivid counter-revolutionary statement. If you used a steel knife to kill a man, his head would roll nicely off on to the ground. To be killed with a wooden knife meant a man had to endure prolonged suffering. When the small group struggled against Zhu Zhenbang, he stayed seated on his bunk, his 'home'. His legs were crossed in front of him, but even crossed like that they shook.

'Stand up!' the head of the small group, Heh Cheng, yelled at him.

'Group Leader, I'm hungry. I can't stand up.' His eyelids moved slowly up and down. 'As soon as I'm up, my legs tremble too much.'

My job was to record the proceedings, but I did not record a single word of any value. The group was full of vehement denunciations; among them, those of the intellectual convicts were the most strident. Their moment had come, their time to assert authority. 'When you criminal convicts do hard labour, you're pretty tough. But now watch out for *us*!'

Intellectual convicts could find an excuse for attack in utterly unreasonable things. For example, Su Xiaosu, against whom I too wrote a large-character poster, was the most honest and honourable of peasants. He had no idea why he had been locked up inside the camps. During a small-group session, when he was vigorously defending himself and swearing that he would do his best to reform, he said, 'I had heard about the Gates of Hell before, but only now do I realize that there is also

126

a Gate to the World. It's even tougher to get through the World Gate than the Gates of Hell.'

In Chinese, the Gate to the World sounds the same as worldview, an important concept in socialist ideology. Intellectuals in the group immediately clamoured, 'He's intentionally mixing it up. He's debunking the socialist worldview.'

'He's viciously defiling the Reform Policy of our Party that seeks to use a worldview to change people . . .'

'This kind of twisting of concepts has always been a despicable method used by class enemies . . .'

In unison, the intellectuals showed off their knowledge. Some cited quotations and references, others attacked by using innuendoes, but all the while this pitiful farmer didn't understand a word. In fact his understanding or lack of it didn't matter – the only thing that counted was that the Troop Leader heard the commotion.

(Many years later, I read a eulogy written in honour of the revolutionary Shu Beili. This eulogy said that on his deathbed the last thing Shu Beili said was, 'I have no regrets about dying. The only thing I regret is that I have not yet completely reformed my worldview . . .' On reading this, I suddenly remembered this peasant's words. A World Gate really is tougher to get through than the Devil's gate!)

Regrettably, the Troop Leader did not often patronize the small-group meetings. As a result, big-character posters had to be written and pasted to the doors of the barracks. Every day, going to and from work, one could see these so-called 'posters' stuck to the doors in the compound, announcing to the Troop Leader and to all the convicts just who this particular small group was vigorously attacking and denouncing today.

I use the words 'so-called' because the big-character posters of the labour camps were truly unsightly. Big-character posters are a speciality of China. They were born in 1957 (I don't know whether they were used during the Yenan days or not), and grew rapidly until in 1966 they had become all-conquering giants. In 1960, still in their youth, they stumbled into the labour reform camps. Like the convicts inside, they too seemed to become sick and malnourished. In the camps, it did not matter what kind of paper you wrote big-character posters on. A square of toilet paper the size of a man's fist was as good as anything for criticizing someone. When the Group Leader ordered us to criticize this peasant who could not distinguish between a devil's gate and a worldview, I used a piece of scrap paper picked up by the side of the road. Those who had pens used pens; those who didn't used pencils. Anything was fine, so long as it could scratch out a few words.

There was no glue to paste these posters up with – that sort of delicacy would have been eaten long ago. People mostly used the snot from their noses. Some scraped the plaque off their teeth and spread it on the back of the paper. They would pat it up on the wall and that would be that. The lifetime of this sort of big-character poster was no longer than one day.

Just because intellectuals were better at writing posters and giving speeches than common labourers did not mean that the people running the labour camps felt they had a higher 'consciousness'. One sentence spoken by an intellectual could get him in trouble, if it was 'grabbed on to' by someone as a pretext for attack. The intellectual would then be in a much more perilous situation than the target he himself had been criticizing.

To use a saying at the time, 'If you can't eat what we're dishing out now, put it in your pockets, 'cause you're going to eat it sooner or later.'

Yet, oblivious to the damage they were inflicting on themselves, intellectuals were tireless in their denunciations of others. This must be because tragedy is their birthright.

Generally, I quite enjoyed the company of criminal convicts who had a working-class background. They might steal from you, take food out of your very mouth, but they didn't give a damn about what you said. It was extremely rare to have a criminal convict report on you, to have him reveal any counter-revolutionary statements you might have made. These men did not speak up much in meetings – they would lie back on their 'homes' and take a nap. When I pulled up the good sprouts, it was the intellectuals who most vociferously denounced me and called for me to be punished. Group Leader Heh Cheng, for example, was an engineer. This engineer gave a copy of the petition to punish me to Zhu Zhenbang, and asked him to sign his name. Zhu Zhenbang snorted at it in contempt:

'Group Leader, tell 'em we talked about it and leave it at that! We'll punish whoever we feel should be punished ourselves! No point in it. You take it easy now.'

The engineer said he had to sign his name.

'But I don't know how to write!' he countered.

The engineer got mad. 'When you go to fetch things and you have to sign your fucking name for them, you manage it, don't you?'

'Ai! You know I'm so stupid. Sometimes I can write and sometimes I can't!'

With no way out, all the engineer could do was say, 'Well, do you agree or not that he should be punished? If you agree, I'll sign your name for you.'

At that point, Zhu Zhenbang grinned in my direction and said, 'I agree that he should pull even more sprouts out for us to eat in the future!'

Although in the end the Group Leader signed Zhu's name to the petition anyway, it always took some persuading to convince this kind of criminal convict that such and such a person should be punished or criticized. But intellectuals, as soon as they sniffed the direction of the wind, would promptly take up their pens.

Most of the ten men who were arrested in the rewards-and-punishments meeting were this kind of criminal convict. The arrested men and the 'graduates' all stood in the threshing ground in front of the Chairman's platform. The men receiving the reward of graduation stood to the left. Those being punished by being arrested stood to the right. This was to mark a clear division between them. But there was not that much difference between the expressions of the arrested criminal convicts and those of the lucky fellows being graduated.

The arrested men had stolen, looted, tried to escape, agitated, 'played dead dog', abused the Troop Leader . . . they had committed every conceivable crime in the camp. Now their wish was fulfilled, as they left for the green pastures that they had wanted to go to from the beginning. They were going to be punished by being made regular convicts, with regular hours.

The thirteen graduates, lucky bastards, were nothing more than some KMT soldiers and petty officers. Most of them held the title of bao-head and jia-head.* These men had already been reformed in the labour camps for five or six years. After graduation, they couldn't go back to their homes, their real homes. All they could do was stay on this farm as workers, like the orderly, the chef for the Old Commissar who ate the public ducks every day. The camps needed this kind of technically experienced labour.

On this occasion, one of the men graduating was an old convict named Wang who had been my Group Leader in the past. He had been a bao-head in the Old Society. His face was completely covered in wrinkles. He tried his best to be a responsible Group Leader, and he led the way in every kind of hard labour. He was my first teacher in how to do farm work – if I had still been in his group, I would never have committed the embarrassing mistake of pulling up good beets. From the start, he would have told me how to thin out the sprouts. The work he had to do as Group Leader was both exhausting and exasperating, since after finishing work in the fields he was often required to hold meetings with the Troop Leaders.

As a result, he was always taking naps during the day. He would close his eyes even while eating. Every time he chewed, his eyes would flutter a little, showing frighteningly white eyeballs. He only had to hear the Troop Leader calling his name, however, and he would immediately wake up, even in the dead of night. He would roll out of bed and bound to wherever the Troop

*The bao-jia system was organized on the basis of households – each jia had ten households and each bao had ten jia or a hundred households. This was defined as 'a system by which the KMT reactionary clique enforced its Fascist rule at the primary level after 1932 . . .'

Leader was, to stand at respectful and erect attention before him.

Is this what could be called having properly reformed? Was he, then, a model graduate? I didn't see a shred of happiness on his face as he prepared to graduate. Standing there, he was still just like some sleeping bug. When we heard the camp leader (the very one that I later discovered was carrying on a romance with the actress) say that 'graduating is not the conclusion of reform, it is the beginning of continuing to reform', he looked as though he wanted to fall over and let the earth cradle him for a long sleep.

13 August
Farm Twelve thinned sugar-beet sprouts. Troop Leader Yue oversaw the work. Evening struggle-and-criticism session against Fang Aihua.
14 August
Pulled weeds at Canal Three. At evening rollcall Troop Leader Yue made a report. Was about problems that have begun to appear (escaping, stealing).
15 August
Cut grass at Canal One Evening Old Commissar made a report (problems of everyday hygiene).
16 August
Cut grass at Canal One.
17 August
Morning cut grass at Canal One, afternoon pulled up grass with the small group. Evening saw movie *Youth in Battle*. Got allocated one jin of muskmelon.

I was thinning sugar beets again.

No policemen or guards watched over us as we worked, but the Troop Leader would oversee us, like a herdsman herding his sheep. He had to assign work responsibilities, examine and supervise what we did, reprimand those who were laggards and praise those who were doing well. In addition to these management tasks, he also had to guard us.

Being Troop Leader for education-through-labour convicts was much harder than being Troop Leader in an ordinary labour reform camp. In a regular labour reform camp, the responsibilities of guards and management cadres were separate. This led to the marvellous situation that guards didn't care if field work ever got done or not. When it was time for *them* to go home, they rounded up the convicts and everyone went home. Cadres doing the management were responsible only for the work and the 'thinking' of the convicts – they were not in charge of guarding them.

In our case, everything was swept into one basket.

All the management cadres were under the jurisdiction of the Labour Reform Bureau, and they were all demobilized army men. The one I specifically mention in the diary on this day was a demobilized army man named Troop Leader Yue.

Every day, one or another Troop Leader would lead us convicts out to work: why did I make a point on this day of saying who the Troop Leader was?

On 13 August, off we went again to the sugar-beet fields. The convicts naturally remembered the day when I had made such a fool of myself here. No matter how

135

many times this sort of thing happened to others, when I played the role it seemed to make the men particularly merry. I was tall and thin, bare-headed, with high cheek-bones and hollow cheeks, and on my chin was a fuzz of downy fur that had never been shaved. I wore a pair of old broken glasses that used cotton cloth ties instead of side-pieces – these hooked around my ears to keep the glasses on. The cotton cloth pulled my ears forward to become what was commonly called 'wind-catching ears'. The glasses had a strip of white rubber stuck on the bridge of the nose, just like the white nose of a clown.

When we got to the field, the big talkers among the convicts began a vivid description of the comic scene that had occurred. Some even mimicked my posture – the string of sugar-beet sprouts around my 'dog's neck', the way I staggered forward, back bent like a camel.

Troop Leader Yue saw it all, standing on top of the big canal, and he too began to laugh. After a while, he walked over to me and gave me a friendly pat on the shoulder.

'You dog,' he said, 'count yourself lucky. If you'd run up against me that day, not only would I have made you parade around with sugar beets hanging from you, you dogshitter, I would have made you eat every one!'

This was another rare chance for some entertainment, and the convicts all howled with laughter. 'That would have been exactly what he wanted. No matter how many sugar-beets you loaded him with, he'd have eaten them all!'

'Hell! If he didn't, he could leave some for me!'

'Right, pull up some more today! Pull a few extra so we can all eat together . . .!'

The convicts were an extremely sensitive herd of animals – this was their most lovable point. There was nothing much to say, but they would pitch in anyway to get the cameraderie going. I thought back to my performance that day – maybe it really was almost as good as Charlie Chaplin. At the very least it was a caricature of Don Quixote. Eventually I couldn't help laughing myself.

Troop Leader Yue's pat on my shoulder invisibly erased the problem. My mistake was no longer considered such a crime, so there was no need to punish me for it. Just as Zhu Zhenbang had said: 'Let us say a little something and forget it!' The report to which the entire group had signed their names demanding that I be punished could not stand up to that one little pat from Troop Leader Yue.

And so that night I felt honoured by his pat as I wrote in my diary. Troop Leader Yue was a good man. Unfortunately the good ones were the ones who didn't live long. When I went into the camps the second time, he and the old convict named Wang were no longer around. I asked about them, and learned that they had passed away. Those who reform others and those who are reformed themselves move towards the same common end.

Yes, I was still able to laugh. I could even consider a tap on my shoulder by the Troop Leader as a special honour. People had already begun to regard the ridiculing of others as a means of education, so it was natural that people became thick-skinned and shameless. After ridicule became a proper and indeed popular method of education in China, we turned into a people that could not be shamed. After many years of this, we are now discovering that a nation of people that is unable to feel shame is a nation that jeopardizes its future.

And yet, it was precisely because I could laugh along with everyone else that I am living today. My ability to laugh was because I had long experienced being criticized, being attacked and struggled against. It was because I had already spent more than seven hundred days of training in the labour reform camp. I had been through the gradual process of 'heat treatment', as they say in steel refining. If I had come up against the experience of being paraded with a string of beets around my neck in normal life, I would have committed suicide in a minute. Indeed, six years later there were many people a generation older than I who, as they later said, 'died without being cleared of false charges'. These people, who died by their own hands, were 'pressured until death'.

Their deaths could be blamed on the fact that they had not had a taste of the feeling before. They were unable to turn ridicule of others into self-mockery. Among those who killed themselves because they couldn't endure ridicule, many had aggressively criticized others in 1957, had 'exposed a few facts'. (Exceptions included Fu Lei,* and a few other rightists.) One can imagine their shock and anger when the treatment they had grown accustomed to meting out to others was turned on themselves.

In the evening, it was again 'evening rollcall'. 'Troop Leader Yue made a report.' The diary entries preceding this had noted many reports, many rollcalls, but in them

*Translator of Balzac and a highly respected scholar, who committed suicide.

I only included one main point; in some of them I neglected to add even that. This was because those reports seemed to have no main point – as the Old Commissar had arranged so well, they were simply to keep us from resting.

By now, all I remember about them is the sky above, that mesmerizing expanse of starry sky above the threshing ground. On a summer's night, the constellations glistened. The Milky Way seemed to flash across the sky. The heavens were brilliant, even without a moon. People enter a kind of dream state when they are extremely exhausted. Listening to the curses and denunciations over and over again, I simply put my head back and released my spirits, allowing them to float out to the ends of the universe. Gazing up at the starlit sky from a labour reform camp, the contrast between human insignificance and the vastness of the universe became even more powerful. One could not help but wonder why, in such a vast, boundless world, one stood on such a tiny place – and why it was mandated that one should be anchored to this place.

And so . . . escape. Most who dared to attempt escape were criminal convicts. Intellectuals who escaped were extremely rare. I escaped once, towards the end of 1959, and set what was then an unprecedented example among intellectual convicts. The events of my fifteen days during that escape are the subject of another story; I don't intend to describe them here. After escaping I came back of my own volition – as a result, I was not punished. The event did not result in an 'elevation' to the paradise that everyone yearned for, the ranks of regular convicts.

The main reason the Group Leader tried to mobilize

the men to get me punished for pulling up sprouts was because I had attempted this early escape. He was adding my sprout crime to that previous crime: you can't blame him for trying to make a big deal out of something small.

Although camp leaders often told us that living conditions of people outside were even worse, that they had even less to eat, stubborn-headed criminal convicts would still try to find ways to get out. (This kind of inducement to get convicts not to escape set a precedent, I fear, for prison management in other countries. It was always 'The life of a man at large is not as good as that of a prisoner'!) Since men kept escaping, we kept holding meetings to criticize and attack them. We called their names in rollcalls and gave 'reports'. We would joke among ourselves as they counted the men: 'Who's not here? Would those not here please raise their hands!'

Those who had escaped were long gone; those left behind were the ones who endured the criticism, the curses, the attacks.

I've been told that the night I escaped the troop was very tense for a while. Station Head Four, leader of that most primitive Station where I was posted, was furious. 'That big little rightist's escaped, God damn it!'

The 'big' indicated my status as the only rightist to have been specified by name in the Party's organ, the *People's Daily*. The 'little' was because I was the youngest convict. All of the intellectuals in Station Four were subjected to haranguing that night, after which they were searched. The practice of mutual surveillance was then tightened up. This is probably one reason many intellectual prisoners were not very happy with me.

On 14 August, Troop Leader Yue ferociously cursed a

different convict who had escaped, not me. It seemed that escapes were on the rise. If you had not seen friends you knew well for several days, that meant that either they were dead or they had escaped – there was no other possibility. It was not conceivable that they might have graduated and slipped away without letting you know. Graduation involved holding a graduation ceremony, namely a punishments-and-rewards meeting. This was a large-scale group affair. It wasn't done in a piecemeal way, since none of us had individual prison sentences.

Escaping from the camps was supremely easy. Since our punishment was considered the highest level of 'administrative' punishment, not criminal punishment, not only did we not have guards watching over us, there were no high walls and steel-mesh fences to hold us in.

The prisoners' compound was like the compound in a regular public apartment building. It was surrounded by a wall no more than four feet high, made of earthen bricks and mud. A dog could have jumped over it. (The second time I was in the camps was during the Great Cultural Revolution, and by then the walls had been raised to six feet, with barbed wire added to the top.)

Around one hundred Troop Leaders, with only two hundred eyes, had to watch over several thousand convicts. As a result, we were as free as the wind – we could practically walk out of the camps right under the nose of a Troop Leader.

How were they to handle this problem? Naturally there were ways. The best was to rely on the self-policing of the convicts themselves. The most trusted people in the camps were convicts who had committed political mistakes, namely 'historical counter-revolutionaries' and 'rightists'. These were the people who are generally referred to as political prisoners. The background of these convicts, including level of education, degree of morality, management experience, even 'thought consciousness' or political awareness, tended to be much more elevated than that of your normal Troop Leader. If you classified them by the common categories right and left, they would be left of the Group Leaders, but they would never be right of a Troop Leader.

For example, the Troop Leader who paraded me around let it go after that – he forgot about it. The engineer who was our Group Leader, on the other hand, kept it firmly in mind. As soon as I came back he drafted a petition to have me punished. After hearing about this, Troop Leader Yue warmly slapped me on the back. Would the engineer have done that? He was aching to get at me, to break me. If the leader I mentioned before, with such a Confucian air about him, had been Group Leader – just think, could he possibly have been less efficient than the labour reform camp cadres? He would have managed our group beautifully, making every man docile and obedient.

The camps had loads of men like the engineer for Group Leaders, and this constituted an internal network of control, a form of management. As for surveillance, for eyes, there were several thousand convicts and so there were several thousand pairs of eyes. Mutual surveillance, mutual exposure, mutual investigation – these are the most potent form of control. That's why there are so many references to big-character posters in my diary, also to small-group meetings, thought critiques, etc. All these things were calculated to keep us on edge, to keep us behaving.

For example, on 2 August I've noted that there was a

double exposing of others. Dishing up one portion was not enough – one had to expose two! This was a duty, it was a responsibility that had to be carried out, or else. What happened if you failed? Well, that showed that you hadn't paid enough attention to the actions and words of others. It meant that, after today, you'd better open your eyes and your ears. If you did not, the leaders would harangue you, make a 'report' to you, virtually every night. But most important, how many people you exposed and 'investigated' was a large factor in whether or not you could graduate.

The leaders of the camps were also aware that there was hardly any place to which you could escape. The reports that they made were not so far off: during those months and years, conditions outside the camps often really were even worse than inside. The distinction was between a very large prison and a relatively small prison. There was a tight network of surveillance everywhere.

Those who had been officially released were still considered released-convicts-from-labour-reform-and-labour-education – why not just say 'escaped prisoner'! You had to show your identity if you wanted to buy a bus ticket. Or to stay in a hotel. You had to produce your identity card to buy a box of matches. Sleeping in the open air was out of the question – it was dangerous because it was suspicious. And you certainly could not wander around any village alone. Every single person belonged to a commune, a large troop or a small troop, so how was it that you were out travelling on your own? Why did you have this strange leisure and freedom to kick around by yourself?

And if you went home, you brought sudden fear to your family, even terror. Then too, for rightists there was always the confounding question, 'Now that you have been reformed, now that you've graduated, what exactly are you going to do?' Not a single rightist was able to go out and grab the carrot, jump over the traces and leave the cart behind. As a result, those who had no special reason to, or no special courage, were incapable of escaping. I could be considered one of those who contravened the norm. Yet my courage in trying to escape came simply from my greater fear of dying.

At that time, a very young rightist was sleeping beside me. He was only a few years older than I. He too was tall and thin, and from the outside he really looked more or less like me. The difference was that he had a very pink complexion, and broad and fleshy lips. Moreover, white spit would accumulate at the corners of his mouth. He rarely spoke. Generally, he was even more exhausted than I was, so tired that he wouldn't take the trouble to do up his belt or his shoelaces. When we were hauling dirt with the back-baskets, he would automatically move on after someone had shovelled in just one shovelful of dirt. No matter how the person packing the dirt yelled to him to come back, he wouldn't even turn his head. Dumping the dirt at the other end, he would let it slump out, then straighten his back and, like a donkey kicking its heels, kick the basket back up on his back. While doing this, his gloomy, vacant eyes would be gazing out at some distant place. Only after a long, long time would he sluggishly walk back for more. On the return route, he would seemingly be thinking, or savouring the vistas that he had just been gazing at. When it was the practice in the camp to make yourself a kind of face mask to keep off mosquitoes, he would leave it on even while he was working. If you looked carefully, under the netting you could see that his eyes were closed.

People called him an idiot. Only I had some slight understanding that he had cordoned off his entire being, that after removing himself from the world he found he could enjoy living in a dream state. I would have liked to follow his example, but I couldn't. It required an incredibly resolute determination to cast off the world. If one had the slightest lingering desire or care, then it was impossible to achieve that state.

There was no one with whom he could really talk. He never said anything to me, even though he slept right next to me. If he happened to press against me when he turned over, he seemed to be unaware of it. When I pressed against him he didn't care in the slightest. He certainly would never say, 'Please pull your legs back,' or anything like that. Dinner was taken 'home' and eaten there after work. Everyone would take his grass soup and, very carefully, carry it to his place on the kang. Each curled up on his own bedding. Spoonful by spoonful, we would each slowly savour our meal. My custom was to eat while I read an old newspaper, trying my best to extend the pleasurable experience of 'eating'.

Despite this, he managed to eat more slowly than I did. This made me terribly jealous. If there were no group meeting on a particular evening, and he had not gone to listen to reports, he could make one portion of grass soup last all the way from getting off work to going to sleep. His method was to observe each spoonful of soup very thoroughly before eating it, as though he was trying his utmost to see the former green-jade succulence that had been cooked out of the weeds in the process of making the soup. Not until he could clearly see that phantom colour would he put the spoonful into his mouth. After putting it in his mouth he would lightly, gently chew that one spoonful of watery soup. Only when every part of his mouth had enjoyed its moistness would he allow the liquid to go into his stomach.

In this manner, he could make each spoonful of soup last for one hundred years.

If we had the good fortune to be issued dry rations for a meal, such as a steamed bun or rice, he would first use his spoon the divide the food into tiny portions. The steamed bun would be made into kernel-sized bits. Each small portion then seemed to become as difficult to chew as bones. Chewing bones was naturally more difficult than chewing soup – it couldn't be accomplished without several hours of valiant effort.

He only ever said one thing to me that was interesting. He said, 'I . . . like . . . to eat watery things. I . . . don't . . . like . . . to eat dry things.'

My god! The man was so hungry that the skin of his belly was practically sticking to his spine, and yet he could say that he preferred watery soup to real food.

Perhaps it was because of his high moral standing, or perhaps it was simply out of laziness, but he never 'ate greens', and he never traded for food. On a rare day of rest, people rushed in and out like mad, making a market like at a county fair. But he buried his head in his stinking bedding, looking like some kind of hump-backed bird. His two thin, dry legs, sticking out at the other end, seemed exceptionally long. He still had things he could have traded. He had a leather case that appeared to be packed full, but he never once opened it. This also meant that he never changed his underwear. When we were reassigned to a different group, when we 'moved house', that leather case became an encumbrance to him.

The Troop Leader would never look after this kind of idiot – he would certainly never let him put his luggage on the cart. Plus he had no friends, so there was no one to help him. With that remarkably good-looking leather case on his back, it was three steps and a gasp, two steps and a pant. He was always the last one to reach a newly assigned place.

Why had he come to do labour reform? What had his position, his background been? What kind of crime had he committed? No one in the group knew. One day when it rained, the convicts were all together in the barracks plaiting rope, and a question came up about the position of a certain constellation. This was in the context of a discussion about escaping. I suddenly heard him mutter to himself:

'In Babylonian times, astronomy was already quite developed.'

Amazed, I turned to look at him, but he did not say anything else.

It was from his face that I first learned to recognize a 'death mask'. In addition to those characteristics that I have described above, his whole body emanated a particular stench. His face was a dark shade of red, it looked like a piece of filthy dirty cloth that has been left in the garbage heap. I didn't pay much attention at the time, thinking that this was the result of his extreme lack of hygiene. But who wasn't dirty? Was I so much cleaner than he was?

This kind of person was naturally a prime target for attack in the small group. He slept beside me, and his only benefit to me was that he served as a shield. With him near by, my faults were not so apparent.

He seemed to be an intellectual, but he did not speak at all during meetings. This species of intellectual was extremely rare in the camps, sighted about as often as a unicorn. Generally speaking, a meeting was an opportunity for intellectuals to put their special abilities on display. During these times, discussion would be especially shrill, and the criticism and attacks on others would become sharp and biting. Our few days of not working rarely fell on a Sunday. None the less, every Sunday men became like worshippers going to church – on that night it was obligatory to hold a meeting to scrutinize one's daily living.

In each small group on Sunday evening, convicts would sit cross-legged on their bunks, and, like true believers, confess their sins. They would tell of mistakes they had committed during the week, mistakes they now regretted.

Who really believes that he personally has made mistakes? It was much easier to consolidate all the sins and put them on somebody else, so that everyone could get the fireworks going in order to 'help him'. It was at times like this that the man who slept beside me became an ideal target.

Someone would say, 'The Party wants us to establish socialism as expeditiously as possible. But this guy comes along with his "fewer, slower, poorer and more costly". He intentionally sings a counter-revolutionary tune to our great Party . . .'

Someone else would say, 'We shouldn't be deceived by what he looks like on the outside. Never saying a word and all. In fact, that's one of the most vicious tricks used by class enemies against the proletariat. The Great Leader told us from the beginning, when times are not opportune for them, class enemies will always lie down and play dead . . .'

'Do you know what he believes?' somebody else would laugh in a sinister way. 'You don't, right?! Because he never reveals himself. Those who don't talk are most full of hatred for the Party, for socialism. It's not that he doesn't speak because he doesn't have anything to say – if the American imperialists and the KMT counter-attacked, I guarantee he would have more to say than anyone . . .'

I kept the minutes of the meeting. Keeping minutes had the virtue of allowing you to say less, or nothing at all. I always wrote as slowly as possible. When the speaker finished, I would pretend that I was still writing what he had said. Minutes had to be written under the light of a lamp, though, sitting in the most visible place. One couldn't hide in the shadows, like some others, curled up into as small a presence as possible. When awkward silence descended on the meeting, the Group Leader could always remember that there was still some-one, me, who hadn't spoken.

'Hey! You! Tell us what you think! You sleep beside him, after all. What kind of behaviour have you noticed that isn't proper? Has he said anything counter-revolu-tionary?' During the last meeting, the Group Leader dis-covered me and indicated that I had better speak up.

I still had a degree of self-awareness, and I felt that the idea that these convicts considered themselves to be proletariat was ludicrous. I myself was humble enough to believe that I didn't dare count as proletariat, although I was also not willing to be 'capitalist'. Since we ourselves were not proletariat, how could he be considered our enemy? If not us, then of which class was he the enemy? It was difficult to say anything before coming to terms with my own position on all this.

None the less his way of eating was, undeniably, annoying. Every single evening his eating habits would drive me crazy. So far as I was concerned, his noiseless existence was like the loudest racket. There was no reason in the world that I should protect him – it might not be a bad thing to take this opportunity, as they say, to throw stones on him while he was down in the well. Didn't I too have to 'represent' myself well, to make a good impression?

And so, after clearing my throat for a while, I said, 'When he eats . . . well, he intentionally dawdles. It takes him half a day to finish a meal. I think there's something funny about that . . . some problem there.'

It should be said that an unwillingness to appear foolish is probably a common ailment of all mankind. Even in exposing someone, there is a desire to show that you know something others don't know. This does not necessarily mean that one has a specific grudge. It was, therefore, with the greatest difficulty that I kept myself from revealing that sentence he had uttered: 'I . . . like . . . to eat watery things, I don't . . . like . . . to eat dry things.' I knew that although this had a specific meaning for him, to someone else's ears it would gain a very different significance. Specially, it would indicate that he was 'viciously holding our Party's grain in contempt, using food to ridicule our Great Leader's enlightened strategy of substituting-gourds-and-greens-for-lowered-rations'.

Whoever heard of a man who liked to drink watery

things and didn't want to eat proper food? Except for someone who had an intestinal disease, of course.

Since my exposé carried within it a small bit of seemingly factual evidence, it aroused some of the intellectual convicts to further reflection.

'Say, that's right! When this bastard is eating, what's he really thinking? . . .'

'I think that when he intentionally dawdles over his food, he's brazenly saying to the Party in a silent way, "So you give me such a small amount to eat? Well I'll show you! I'll make it look as though I'm eating a lot!" '

Someone then began to criticize him viciously in a low voice. 'Right! Slowly tasting the flavour – isn't that just like a petit bourgeois! Still thinking he's in a high-class restaurant dining for pleasure! If we don't reform it out of people like him, who else?!'

I am not exaggerating this. You don't believe it? Even today, thirty years later, all over China you can still find this sort of person, capable of performing this kind of 'deep analysis'. And, regrettably, this sort of person is generally someone with an education.

The young man remained silent. No matter how you analysed, criticized, attacked or 'helped' him, he did not defend himself. He was eternally immersed in his own world. I have every confidence that his world was the exact opposite of the reality around him. But then, who could know?

Fortunately, the convicts criticizing him only wanted to represent themselves in a good light. They didn't necessarily want to force him into this or that position. When it was time for the meeting to break up, everyone finished his spiel, turned in to bed and went to sleep. Unlike others who were criticized, who would express their bitter determination to reform the major faults that had been revealed, he simply pulled aside his oily bedding and crawled inside. As he did, he gave me a very indistinct but definite smile. Or was he crying? In any event, I saw one corner of his mouth give a little twitch.

The Group Leader looked over the minutes of the evening's discussion: the pages were densely filled with words. That looked fine. It would satisfy the Troop Leader.

The next day was Monday. As usual, it was not yet light when we stumbled out of bed. We immediately went to have breakfast, without rinsing our mouths or washing our faces (I abandoned such capitalist practices as face-washing between 1958 and 1976). But he, in an unprecedented display of opposition, did not get up. His head stayed buried inside the bedding.

Without him, we were not allowed to get anything to eat. Our entire group of eighteen men had to be together, lined up before the window of the kitchen, before breakfast could begin. First there would be a tally of all the men: if one were absent, the cook would not feed any of us. The fact of his absence soon became obvious, and the Group Leader ordered me to go wake him up.

'Huh! So this bastard thinks he can play dead dog? Forget it! Drag him out!'

Half awake myself, I went back to shake him. His body gave with my shove, but he still didn't make a sound. I then pulled back his bedding but when my hand connected with his body I had a strange sensation. Shocked, I cried out.

'Group Leader, he's stiff!'

As the Great Helmsman* once said, 'Dying is quite a frequent occurrence.' Hearing my shout, the Group Leader was not at all alarmed. He just gave a 'humph!', then brought in a flashlight. (Electricity had still not reached the labour reform camp – kerosene lanterns were used for light. Each small group was issued one flashlight, which was under the control of the Group Leader.) He crawled up beside the silent man to take a look. After touching his body, he said calmly, 'OK, so we forget him. We'll go and eat first.' With that, he made his bed and told the others to line up under the kitchen window.

This Group Leader belonged to the variety of criminals called 'historical counter-revolutionary elements'. He had once been a company commander in the Kuomintang Army and was a graduate of the Whampoa Academy in its later years. I couldn't help but admire his mettle, his military discipline in turning such a blind eye to death. When the remaining seventeen men in the group lined up at the kitchen window, the Group Leader reported to the cook that one of the bastards was sick, and couldn't come for his meal. Naturally, the cook had to believe the Group Leader, and so as usual he ladled out eighteen portions of the watery soup that the dead man had liked so much. Without caring about whether they liked it or not, the Group Leader split the extra portion between two criminal convicts who were particularly good workers.

The Group Leader's quiet demeanour was contagious – sixteen men silently ate the soup in their bowls. Two of them, the criminal convicts, were quite pleased with the situation. Only I was unable to make the food go

*Mao Zedong.

down. It seemed to have become a bowl of the white spit that always settled at the corners of his mouth.

When the Group Leader came to have a look at him, I took advantage of the light from his torch to glance at the man's face. Apart from the death mask that I had grown accustomed to seeing, I noticed with horror that long hairs had grown out overnight. His thick, heavy lips were wide open, and the eyes that so loved to gaze over the scenery stared out. Under the light of the torch, he seemed to be searching in all directions, all the while shouting, 'Babylon! Babylon!'

It was in that moment that the thought of escaping came to me. That twitch of the mouth that he gave me just before dying – I'll never be sure if he was contemptuous of me, reproaching me or thanking me. How responsible was I for his death? The question plagued me, to the extent that I never again felt innocent and naïve.

After returning from my escape, I saw many more corpses – death became commonplace. Later I came to be just like the graduate of the Whampoa Military Academy, but even more brave. Once, in a heavy rain, when I had picked up my soup and was carrying it back to the barracks, so that on the way it was in danger of becoming even more watery, I ducked into an empty earthen shed near by. I figured that I would stay out of the downpour while I ate my precious meal. It turned out that the room was occupied by a convict who had just died. He was stretched out like the character for 'big' on the door that had been removed for the purpose. I very politely moved one of his arms aside, asking if he could make a little room. Then I sat down beside him to finish my still-warm soup.

I had been reformed to the extent that I could share a

room with any ghost, especially as I had shared a night on a sixty-centimetre-wide bunk with a stiff that grew long hairs overnight.

Oh Babylon! Babylon! My Babylon!

20 August
Morning pulled grass at Canal One. Afternoon dug vegetables at Canal Two. Received letter from *Ningxia News* rejecting 'Aerial' manuscript.

21 August
Farm Sixteen thinned sugar-beet sprouts. Rested half-day in the morning, rained suddenly at four in the afternoon, stopped work.

In evening Group Leader Zhao Ying assigned me to write material, reflecting currently existing problems in the leadership of the small group. Wrote Mother a letter, asking her to mail some food. Spent two jiao to buy half an ear of corn and one-third of a gourd.

22 August
Morning pulled grass at Canal Two, afternoon bundled grass. Material on small group finished and handed over to Zhao Ying.

23 August
Got fertilizer from the duck pen. Asked Li Ruzhi to mail letter to my mother. Bought 7 jiao 4 fen worth of tobacco from Li Jingsheng. Borrowed 1 yuan 1 jiao 4 fen from old Zhou (tobacco and gourd).

24 August
Cut grass at Canal Five, Six. Got 3 yuan. Finished pulling grass.

25 August
Farm Eleven thinned sugar beets. Received allocation of 1 jiao worth of cucumbers. (Clear with occasional clouds.)

26 August
Farm Twelve thinned sugar beets and cabbage. Troop Leader Sun reported in the evening, regarding questions to do with the finishing of the grass-pulling work.

27 August
Farm Twelve thinned sugar beets. Assigned to be record keeper for the small group.

My entry for 25 August notes the weather, out of habit: clear with occasional clouds. The entry had no special significance, yet it was this kind of clear sky with occasional clouds that seduced me into wanting to stay alive in the damned world that I was living in. From what I wrote in the diary during this period, the reader can tell that I was still relatively stable – both in terms of my emotional state and in terms of my living conditions. I did not plan to escape again nor did I think of committing suicide. After all, I was still alive, still eating grass soup, and every few days I could get hold of a luxury item such as some salt, a gourd, some tobacco. I even managed to find time to write a few so-called poems. Only one thing kept bothering me, and it was the sky.

Few people on earth can have been so painfully aware of how beauty can torment a man. Yes, even beauty can torment. In the sky, in the interplay between evening light and clouds, in every blade of grass and every branch of a tree, in the course of the growing and final maturity of the crops, in the thawing and once again the freezing of the ground, in every shovelful of the earth I dug . . . in all of these was hidden an inescapable fascination, a temptation. They made it hard for a man to leave this earth lightly. There were no springs here, no tripping brooks, no exotic mountains or fantastic rockeries. Nothing bloomed here except weeds. Even the grasses were plants with absolutely no aesthetic value – dog-tail sedge, reeds and that sort of thing.

And yet, this place had unique spaciousness, boundless reaches, an emptiness which shook a man to the core. The line between heaven and earth was so distinct – the sky was sky, the earth was earth, with only wind passing back and forth between.

At early dawn, the wooden gate of the compound would scrape open against the ground, and we convicts would emerge from the barracks where we had been locked up all night. In those moments, I could barely endure the sudden contrast between the filth inside and the fresh purity of the world outside. We were like travellers who have flown half-way around the world overnight, and find it hard, so suddenly, to adapt.

We would look out over the summer landscape, and see every weed, every grass, every plant absorbing nutrition, growing, thriving. It seemed that man alone was suffering from hunger.

Why was that?

Why?

There was another matter that tormented me, and that was the dividing of things. Striving to be as fair and honest as possible could make one suffer even more.

The diary often notes that on a particular day certain things were allocated: salt, tobacco, watermelon, muskmelon, cucumbers, and so on. Why should such trivialities be included in my record? These items were worth a few cents, or a few tenths of a cent.

Yet the divvying-up and allocating of these things constituted the most important event in our daily lives. After work, on the way home, if we saw a cart parked in front of the camp compound, we would become amazingly cheerful. Bodies that had toiled all day would suddenly liven up. Eyes that gazed out from faces already bearing traces of the 'death mask' would begin to glow with a certain kind of greedy cunning. Hands and feet would begin to shake uncontrollably. Like disturbed ant-hills, the barracks would erupt into action – the only difference was that ants would not call out like the convicts:

'Dividing melons! Dividing melons! . . .'

'Hurry! Quick, get the bag!'

The man on duty from each group would race to get the group's hemp bag. This was considered one of the group's great treasures. Normally it would be folded neatly and tucked safely under the Group Leader's bedding. Now it was shaken out, clamped under an armpit and hurriedly rushed to the line forming by the cart. The Troop Leader or a freed convict (like the middle-school teacher who was in charge of watching over the vegetable cellar) would already be waiting there. Once the man on duty from each group was present, the divvying-up would begin, according to the number of men in each group.

At the cart, the measuring was done with a balance. Once the food was taken back to the small group, however, where was one supposed to find a balance? Eighteen pairs of eyes would be staring at this pile of sustenance, watching to see how fair the division was.

From the time I entered the camps, the responsibility for dividing things up always fell to me. I don't know why. No matter which group I was reassigned to, I was asked to be responsible for the division of food. Convicts in a group never trusted their Group Leader, nor did he ever trust the other convicts. Seventeen pairs of eyes therefore would stare at my pair of hands; some of the men would squat on the ground, some would stand to one side looking sideways through cold eyes. Every motion I made was watched with rapt attention; people vied with one another to give suggestions on how to make the split.

Among the eighteen men there were eighteen different standards of measurement. Splitting up a pile of food was infinitely more difficult than writing a poem. Let us say, for example, that the group had been allocated thirty-six jin of cucumbers. Each man was to get two jin, but without a scale how was it possible to get eighteen identical portions? There are always large cucumbers, small ones, good ones, bad ones, fresh ones and others that are not so fresh. You must take all of these various factors into account. Until you have it worked out so that the entire group nods in approval, you are not allowed to stop. The men are all hungry, their eyes are hungry. I divvy out the portions until my head is spinning and my eyes are blurred, until the sky and earth seem to be floating in cucumbers, like stars, until the Group Leader finally demands of everyone: 'How about it?! Speak up!'

And what does everyone say? Certainly no one says a word of agreement. Ultimately one man makes a small move to grab a cucumber and immediately all are struggling to get their share. In a moment, seventeen small piles of cucumbers are snatched away. Just one, mine, is left there – the one nobody else wanted. An important principle has been agreed upon before the process: the man responsible for splitting the food into equal portions takes his portion last.

Personally I feel that I need a larger portion than anyone. A death mask has already made its appearance on my face, and yet I have to let myself get the worst of the deal. I silently pick up the pile of cucumbers remaining on the ground, one by one, and when I eat them the flavour is often mixed with my tears.

Why was such an important event not specifically described in the diary?

Starting from July 1960, the division of food in the manner described above was not a daily event, and this is reflected in the journal. But from November 1958 until October 1959, I had to endure this torment three times every day.

During that period, when convicts went to get their meals they didn't line up neatly by the kitchen window in their own groups. The cooks did not ladle food directly into each convict's basin. Instead, the men on duty from each small group (for it was always two men, in order to prevent anyone from stealing mouthfuls on the way) would take the food bucket and the water bucket to the kitchen and bring back food and water for everyone. After returning to the barracks, the food would be divided by the convict most trusted by all the rest. The lives of all the groups were tied to the ladle of the cook; and the lives of the men in each group were tied directly to the ladle of the man, namely me, serving out the food.

Whether or not a man kept on living, or whether he was able to live one more day or two, appeared to depend on whether he was given two extra or two fewer grains of rice. One's survival did *not* depend on the vitamins or protein in one or two grains of rice – but it did depend on the spiritual sustenance, the encouragement those grains gave a man. After every convict had received his portion, he would stir it around in his basin a long time, glancing at everybody else's basin and comparing their amounts to his own. If he had received one grain of rice too few – or what he, anyway, regarded as less than others – he would quickly develop the syndrome mentioned above: the wilting sickness.

'I'm getting less than the others! I'm getting less than the others!' How can a man who has this refrain inside him from morning till night not collapse?

The wooden bucket in which the small group hauled its food was another of its treasures. Every man in the group regarded it with love and affection. Never mind that it reeked, that it was sour and filthy from previous meals; never mind that the rope attached to it was slimy with countless watery soups. When the convicts went out to work, or when they switched fields during a workday, the first thing they thought of was making sure to bring the bucket along. It was as though the bucket was more important to them than a child. Yes, for without it you were unable to eat. And if you did not eat you would die.

The man on food duty from each small group had major responsibilities. Among other things, he had to calculate the best time to go to the kitchen to get his group's food. When the cook made a meal, he would pour finished soup from great cooking pots into a wooden keg that was as tall as a man. From this vessel he would then distribute the soup to the small groups, ladling it into their buckets. Groups who arrived at the beginning of this process would naturally get the thinner soup floating on top; those who came later would get the benefit of thicker material that had sunk to the bottom. If you got it just right, you might even find some undissolved lumps of flour.

Each Station, however, had over one thousand men, and so the kitchen needed at least a dozen large wooden kegs for each meal. The small groups did not pick up their food according to any specific order – whichever group's man arrived at any given time got served. The trick was to work it so that you came just at the time when a large keg was reaching the bottom. You certainly wanted to be there before the next keg was started. How to do it? This depended on the talent of the man on food duty.

Relying on this man alone was sometimes not enough – you had to send out one or two scouts to reconnoitre the situation. If it happened to be a particularly good meal, then the entire group would be mobilized. Men would take turns keeping surreptitious watch at the kitchen window. The Group Leader would sit inside the barracks and direct the action. A man who could hold back and not jump the gun, like that graduate of the Whampoa Military Academy, managed it best. He would appear calm, as though he held the security of a million soldiers hidden in his back pocket – convicts would rush in and out, giving him reports, while he sat back looking very much like a figure in a Peking opera. The man on duty, holding the bucket, would wait beside him, ready at any time to make the assault.

When a convict came in to report to the Group Leader that the large keg was just at the right stage, he would, with one word, order the charge and the man on duty would dash out like the wind. Group Leaders who could not restrain themselves, who became even more nervous and agitated than the man on duty, would plunge in and out of the action themselves. They would be mortally afraid of bringing the ultimate misfortune upon their group. These pitiful men generally had the worst luck – the food that came back to their barracks was often the thinnest gruel. The old convict named Group Leader Wang was one of these.

As a result, every time the small groups were reorganized, convicts would enquire carefully into the qualifications of the Group Leader. Did he have this unique talent? If he did, then they would be satisfied, even if he was more severe than the others.

As the convicts put it: 'Follow a wolf and you eat meat; follow a dog and you eat shit.'

Unfortunately, no matter what group I was assigned to, the others always trusted me. After the man on duty had brought in the food, it was always I who was handed the ladle to divvy it up. The ladle had a fixed capacity, which made it easier – each man got one ladle or one ladle and a half. But how many bits of vegetable were there in the soup bucket? How many clumps of rice? There were slight distinctions between each ladle of gruel – some were a bit thicker, some thinner.

I say I was trusted – in fact, this was purely relative. No convict would completely trust any other person. As a result, the men studied every possible means of dividing the food fairly. One method was to have one convict turn his face away and not watch me divide it. Eighteen bowls would be set down on the ground. After I had filled them, dividing as evenly as I could into eighteen portions, he would close his eyes and randomly assign each bowl to a person. 'So-and-so takes bowl number such-and-such,' he would call out, until all the bowls were taken.

People complained about this method, however, since they weren't able to use their own bowls to eat. Another method we tried was as follows: I would very carefully fill a ladle full of soup or rice, and I would hold it there in my hand. Then a convict, whose back was turned to me, would shout out who this ladle was for. That man would bring forward his bowl and get the food. There was a third, and a fourth way – the ingenuity was endless. Among the hundred-odd small groups in the labour reform camp, at least ninety different methods were probably being practised at any given time. Some groups even made themselves their own unique weighing and measuring devices.

When not working, convicts were most interested in exchanging information on these different ways of measuring food. I have seen many different balances and scales made for the purpose. A small branch would be polished until it was as glossy as jade, then fine measuring lines would be carved on it with great mastery. Each mark shone – the thing was so exquisite that a person holding it wouldn't want to put it down. Seeing it, one could believe that these men, scraped clean of everything including freedom, could have made an aeroplane with their own bare hands.

All these different methods were dreamed up by educated minds. Several hundred engineers, agronomists, accountants, professors, also graduates of universities abroad with masters degrees and PhDs, racked their brains in order to make sure that the balances were precisely even. Criminal convicts would never think of these things – they disdained even to try to think up 'rotten ideas'. They could snatch, they could steal – they had their own ways of supplementing inadequate rations.

'What's the bugger up to?' they would sneer from the sidelines as an intellectual tried to figure out some weighing method or other. Methods thought up by those who were unable to steal or snatch, though, who had to rely completely on a one-ladle ration to survive, were the only fair-and-square, honest methods in the camps. When it came to the question of how to divide up food, criminal convicts were not given a say.

The very last half-ladle of thick material from the bottom of the bucket had to be divided evenly into eighteen portions with chopsticks. Never mind that each portion was no bigger than the sand in your eye. When there was nothing left in the bucket but the wetness and the smell, it was given to the man on duty for his pleasure: this was the reward for his running back and forth, the reward for his bringing in the food.

God himself would have found it hard to divide the rations evenly. None the less, if a particular ladleful looked ever so slightly more watery or less in quantity than another, pandemonium would break out in the group. Particularly if the man who had his back to me and was making the call happened to pick the most evil-tempered convict in the lot.

Being considered a trustworthy type by others has been one of the most bothersome things in my life. Far more trouble than making a living and providing for myself. It's not easy to be a fair and upright man! It was much more exhausting to divvy up food than it was to do hard labour. When it was time to eat, not only would my body be shaking from hunger, but my fingers would be shaking from nerves.

As a result of all this, the Old Commissar and the Troop Leader would reiterate in their reports that we convicts had to band together, we had to co-operate. We were warned repeatedly not to fight when food was being split up. The more obstreperous convicts were cursed and warned until they were 'dripping from the head in dog's blood'.

This was the general rule: our leaders would put us in a position in which it was impossible to have any solidarity, and then they would exhort us to 'unite'.

Fortunately, the system of serving food was later reformed. If it had not been, I would not have come back voluntarily when I escaped.

By the time of these August entries in the diary, our main meals were not apportioned in this way, but small things were still divvied up from time to time. Since small groups no longer needed to divide food in the barracks, the home-made balances disappeared, with the result that it became even more important to have a reliable person do the apportioning. I was called upon to be that person, but this did not mean that I was popular in other respects. For example, since I had weeded out good sprouts, which I should not have done, the Group Leader and intellectual convicts were still actively demanding that I be punished. Every man had to grab every opportunity to 'represent himself well'. People who would exploit their own blood brothers' faults as a way to do this would surely not have mercy on some convict whose face had already begun to assume the death mask.

None the less, after the convicts' petition to have me punished was sent to the authorities, there was no official response. Not only was I not punished but, on the afternoon of 27 August, the Troop Leader suddenly announced that I was to be appointed record keeper, or accountant, of our small group. Standing high above on the bank of the canal, he yelled down to all the convicts of the assembled small groups, 'We're going to have him do it! After all, he writes well!'

The record keeper of the small group was roughly equivalent to being its Secretary General!

In the evening, when the convicts were pulling their bedding down to go to sleep, I heard the engineer grumble to the man who was sleeping beside him, 'Just look at that. How am I going to manage now? What am I going to do?'

People considered the worst kind of scum by the bottom rank of leaders are often picked out and elevated by the people on top. Yes, the upper crust of China's leaders often gives the lower-down authorities a hard time. Hugging my sour and smelly bedding, I secretly smiled. I knew that although the articles and poetry I mailed out had not been published – every one had been sent back with a refusal – cadres censoring the mail had definitely read them. And they had reported their findings to the leaders.

From now on, I would certainly have to write more eulogies about the Old Commissar, and mail off more poems like the 'Train', 'Aeroplane' and so on that I had already written.

28 August
Farm Fifteen thinned cabbage. After work Troop Leader Sun called a collective meeting (low productivity, eating seedlings on the sly). In the evening Station Leader Yan did rollcall, and yelled about all kinds of behaviour that broke the rules (stealing, encouraging children to take things for you, low productivity, putting out counter-revolutionary ideas). Small group is going to cut the rations of Fang Aihua. Li Jinlie's steamed bun was stolen; Wang Youdao said it was Zhu Zhenbang. Search. Coughed, unable to sleep. Gave 3 jiao back to Ding Wende, 1 yuan 4 jiao and 4 fen back to Zhou Wenlin, 9 jiao back to Ding Haiji. Feng gave me back 7 fen.
29 August
Farm Sixteen went after chemical fertilizer. Talked about poets' attitudes and methods with Ma Weixiao as we went to work. Asked Ding Wende for tobacco; didn't have any. Everybody talked about things to eat. Zhou found half a rabbit leg, cooked and ate it. Evening: study session, evaluated the people most 'advanced' at pulling grass; did a Thought Line-up.

*A*lthough I had been made Secretary General, I had the feeling that I was not long for this world. Life seemed increasingly distant from me. It was slowly moving from my grasp.

August: a beautiful month. Every day I witnessed a glorious sunrise and sunset. The summer days are particularly long in the north-west. The sky is cloudless, and there's no haze over the earth. There would be a soft breeze blowing against our faces when we set out to work in the mornings, and when we came back a brilliant Big Dipper would be shining above us. The air was so clear and clean it could not have been better. Yet every day, all day long, I was coughing.

It was hard to imagine how such a slender, weak body could manage to put out such violent energy. Every cough racked my entire frame, shaking it as though it were under attack. At times I would cough continuously without being able to catch a breath, so I had to force the coughs back in order to breathe. I was in a state of alert at every moment – the boundary between life and death was no more than the space between an inhalation and an exhalation. I often rubbed the thin bones of my chest, thinking as I did that part of the lungs inside must already have died. The coughing became even more intense at night, so that my chest cavity seemed to have been packed with dynamite – explosion after explosion would erupt from within me.

The next one is going to blow me up, I would think. Unable to sleep, I would raise my head to look at the other convicts around me. There wasn't a single ray of light to see by to confirm this, but I had the feeling that each was like the corpse of Babylon – that from each face were emerging long, long hairs. In the dark, with no blue sky outside, I would lose my sense of where I was. Was I living or already dead?

I therefore began to pay up my various debts. The people to whom I owed money are listed carefully in the diary.

Yet under these conditions I still went out to work as usual, still attended study sessions, listened to 'lessons', still participated in evaluations and the 'Thought Line-up'. I seemed to be less afraid of death than of not being with other men. I did not dare follow the example of the criminal convicts and pretend to be a 'dead dog', simply lie down and refuse to move. What was there to be afraid of? I didn't even think about it – I was afraid of a kind of nameless terror. An inchoate terror was more frightening than one that was concrete, that had a specific cause.

Babylon, that most unreformed of men, was a good example: wasn't he still struggling to go out with the rest of us to work until the last day? Didn't he hold examination-of-lifestyle meetings with us until the end? It seems that intellectuals are mostly afraid of not being the same as other people.

I did not want to die. I think that the principal function of all the materialistic education I received was that it kept me from simply going off and dying. Other than this, it was absolutely useless. If I had believed in some kind of heaven or that a man's soul lived on after death, I would long ago have flown off to the place I most yearned for – the clear blue sky.

But there were also men who were *not* materialists who kept on living just the same. And they lived more carefree lives than I did. Ma Weixiao, with whom I discussed poets' attitudes and their methods on 29 August, was one of them. Actually, what we discussed was not poets' attitudes and their methods, but this is what I had to write in the diary. If I had noted down what he actually told me and it had been discovered, the two of us would have been accused of being 'active counter-revolutionaries'.

This man was a Muslim. He was not very old, but he wore three tufts of hair on his face: two on either side of his mouth, which pointed upward, and one which hung down his chin. The one hanging down was long enough to obscure his throat. His looks reminded me of a picture of an ancient Persian in the illustrated version of *The Thousand and One Nights*. As time went on his face stayed well padded – it held no trace of a death mask. His coffee-coloured eyes were unworried and steady.

He had been sent to do hard labour simply because his father was a senior person in religious circles, and had been the head of a Counter-Revolutionary Collective. Ma had been raised in the atmosphere of an extremely religious household. His education was a religious education. It was necessary, needless to say, to reform the worldview of this sort of man. There was no need for him to have committed a crime in order to excuse it: send him into the camps!

On this particular day, walking to Farm Sixteen, he pulled a pouch of tobacco out of his pocket to entice me. 'Go ahead, roll a cigarette,' he said. Because of the tobacco, I immediately moved up to walk beside him.

When the cigarette was rolled and lit, each of us took a long deep puff. Then he looked over at me and said in a mocking tone of voice, 'You're awfully young to be made a rightist. Who would you say was to blame for such a crime?'

The flavour of the pipe-tobacco leaves was rich and strong. I couldn't help but start coughing. This bum was getting things sent from home all the time – things to eat, things to use. Although his father had been a 'ring-leader of counter-revolutionaries' and had been executed, the excellent reputation of the family in his home territory was not affected. The local people ate less in order to help the remaining family members of their 'ringleader'. And so he ate well, and had the leisure to go around thinking about things like who was to blame. I never so much as gave it a thought.

Blame? I had myself to blame, didn't I? I said this to him with my eyes.

'That's right! You have only yourself to blame!' His face broke out in a wicked-looking smile. 'That's because you're not good! None of you rightists is good. Good repays good, and evil repays evil. That means you!'

I mumbled that I didn't quite understand what he meant, and just kept on smoking and coughing.

'Well look. How is the word "good" written? On top is "beautiful" and on the bottom is a "mouth", right? Other words that have to do with matters of the heart all have a heart as their primary component. Bad has a heart, intention has a heart, wanting has a heart, thought has a heart, feeling has a heart, even fear has a heart. Awareness has a heart . . .

'Now, since "bad" has a heart, by all rights "good" should have a heart too,' he concluded. 'Why is the word most related to matters of the heart different?

'Well, little one, you think about it for a while. When the ancients created our script, they had their reasons!

174

Ah yes, the ancients intentionally refrained from including the word good along with other heart-type matters. They most carefully gave it a mouth instead, and in doing that they made it rather like the word "harm". Harm also has a mouth, and no heart. That is because there is nothing better at harming people than a mouth. That goes for good, and it also goes for harm, and naturally it includes your kind who write things. Is it clear to you now? You understand what good is, why it has a mouth and not a heart? Why I say you rightists are no good?'

What he said did have some truth in it. Other intellectual convicts spent all day spouting political slogans, empty as the leaders themselves. Only a man who had never been involved in political study from the day he was born could use this mode of analysis.

'Why?'

'Why? Because, fundamentally, good does not come from the conscience! Good is expressed by the mouth, it is a thing of the lips, not the heart. The written character for it reflects that.' He still looked slightly wicked. 'So long as what comes from your lips is beautiful, so long as you say nice-sounding things, that is good. It doesn't matter what's in your heart. No matter how beneficent, how beautiful your thoughts are, if they don't come out beautiful on your lips, then they're nonsense, they're useless. What's more, they're harmful. You rightists are a confused lot of maggots! You think that your consciences are helping the Party's rectification, that opening yourselves up is good for the Party!

'And what's the result? A good heart is turned into the guts of a jackass and you are told to get out and do hard labour! Why didn't goodness get a good reward?

No matter how you feel about people, about the Party, no matter how bad your heart is inside and you want everyone to go to hell, your mouth has to be good. You have to say pleasant things, you have to adulate and praise them. If what comes from the lips is good, the heart becomes good too. No matter how good your heart is, if it comes out wrong in your mouth, then it becomes bad. So, little one, you understand?'

I opened my starving eyes as wide as possible and said, 'Even if you want to kill someone, if what you say sounds good, then it turns into good intentions?'

'Right!' The evil look on his face evaporated, as it broke into a supremely satisfied smile. 'Now you comprehend. What good intentions?! There's no such thing as good intentions! All there are is pretty words. Good intentions sound good; what sounds bad is harmful. There's nothing in the world more harmful to people than words and articles that say bad things. Remember it after this. No matter what you're thinking inside, no matter how bad your heart is, make sure your mouth and your pen are beautiful, are beneficent, and then you can be a good person.'

No wonder the well-intentioned criticism, the well-intentioned help, of so many intellectuals helped so many other intellectuals along the road to hell.

But did the world really have no such thing as good? After smoking his excellent, real tobacco – no grass or leaves thrown in – and hearing this theory that I had never heard before, I still had to wonder. What, then, was sincerity? Did the world also have no such thing as sincerity?

Soon the discussion returned, as ever, to the issue of food. There was still a piece of road left until we got to where we were going to work. The road was twisting and narrow, so the convicts split naturally into two lines as they walked along. There was no need to carry shovels to the vegetable fields, but even without having to carry anything in their hands, everyone walked listlessly, as though they would have liked to move two steps backwards for every one forward. A glimmering sunrise shone before us on the horizon, but our troop of men looked as if it was going to a funeral. It would be hard to find a more jarring juxtaposition. The Troop Leader walked at the very end of the line, using his rope to whip any convicts who were playing dead dog. There was no guard doing surveillance at the front of the line, and so we were able to chat as we walked.

Ma didn't believe that the entire country was suffering from natural disaster and that this was the cause of the policy of 'substituting-lowered-rations-with-gourds-and-greens'. He didn't think it was a measure adopted after consecutive years of lowered harvests.

'Nonsense! Deception,' he retorted. 'How can such a huge country, nine-point-six million square kilometres, have natural disasters at the same time on every part of it? The soil of our country is good. If just one province has a good crop it can feed all the rest. Don't you worry, the country has plenty of grain. Yes, they have it, but they aren't bringing it out to feed the people. They want the people hungry!'

I smiled even as I coughed. This sort of thing was too ridiculous. 'How can that be?! What benefit to the country is there in keeping people's stomachs empty?'

'What benefit? Plenty!' With an unfathomable cold smile, he said, 'It's the best way there is of reforming people. Let me tell you a story.

'Long ago, when God was creating man, the angels were all against it. One angel said, "Whatever you do, don't make man. Once you do, his descendants will be fighting each other for ever, accusing each other. The blood will flow like rivers, heaven and earth will never be peaceful again."

'God didn't listen. He said, "I must make a man, and let him represent me in speaking to the people, represent me in managing the world." And so, he moulded a man from a ball of clay, and he called the man Adam. Then he taught him all the names of the myriad things in the universe.

'On the same day, he called the angels together and asked them what this was and what that was. The angels said they didn't know. "You haven't told us, God," they said. "How are we supposed to know?"

'God said, "Well, Adam, you tell us what all these things are!" Naturally, Adam knew and he told them all. When the angels heard this, they said, "Man is stronger than we are!" and they all submitted to him. God said, "Your submission should be expressed in some way: you should prostrate yourselves to him." So they did.

'But there was a god-spirit named Erjajilai who would not submit. He said, "I was made from the essence of fire. This man is merely pinched together out of mud: how can I worship him?" He refused. God was angry, and first threw him into the hell of fire for one thousand years. He did not submit. Then He threw him into the hell of ice for one thousand years, and he still would not submit. In the end, God threw him into the hell of famine, and it wasn't too many years before he cried out, "Help! I can't stand it! I submit! I submit!"

'Later, God put this angel, this god-spirit, in charge of

managing devils. So you see, what has the greatest power – what can make even an angel submit to you? Scorching with fire is no use. Freezing with ice is no use. The best thing to do is to starve a person. All the peasants in this country are being brought into the new world from the Old Society, isn't that right? Every single person has to be reformed, right? How do you reform them? Through thought-training? Political education? There are so many people! More than half the population of China doesn't read or write. Educating them is too huge an enterprise.

'No, only famine works. That's the way. Because every single person on earth has to eat. Even the illiterate have to eat. Only by making the people endure hunger can you make them submit to you, worship you. So you see, don't let Chinese people have full stomachs – keep them hungry and in a few years not just people, even dogs, will be reformed. Every one of them will be as obedient as can be: whatever Chairman Mao says will be right. Not a one will dare refuse to prostrate himself before Chairman Mao.'

Just the day before, the 28th, while calling rollcall, the Station Leader had denounced convicts who engaged in counter-revolutionary talk. The several examples of counter-revolutionary statements that he gave were nothing compared to what I had just heard. The Station Leader's examples were:

'Not being able to shit after eating buns made of heavy millet';
'Man is iron, food is steel, if you miss a dinner, starvation you'll feel';
'The policy under way right now means they want horses to be good horses but they don't want them to eat any grass.'

Even these things were enough to bring on curses and beatings. What Ma had said was enough to get both listener and speaker executed. But he didn't give a damn. He just kept on talking as we walked, his face serious, his eyes strong and steady and his back straight as a rod. Fortunately he didn't wave his hands and arms as he spoke, even though his voice was excited. Convicts walking before and behind us paid no attention, assuming perhaps that we two were dining on spiritual matters.

But I was scared to death. Experience had taught me that saying counter-revolutionary things was a crime, but hearing them was a crime as well. If one heard something like this and didn't report it, then the punishment could be worse than that meted out to the speaker. He had used a pinch of tobacco to entice me to his side, just to make me listen to his speech. These thoughts must have festered inside him for a long time – they were like a great obstruction in his intestines. If he didn't turn them into words and get them out, his belly would burst.

Intellectuals' infatuation with words is like normal people's lust for sex. Both are an instinctive impulse. Indulging one's sexual urge could lead to the problem called 'internal contradictions among the people'. Indulging an infatuation with words was the same. Even with one's wife, one had to practise extreme caution. Like a distilled essence, one small spilled drop might turn into a 'contradiction between the enemy and us'.

Today Ma had released some of his lust for words. His agitated mouth would now be stilled for a while and he could be silent for many days.

He had selected me as the object of his release partly because he had some trust in me. He had also grasped the truth that the more counter-revolutionary one's words were, the safer one would be. Statements that were not counter-revolutionary enough to get one seriously punished were often reported by others. Statements that were definitely serious were reported less often. The statements he had just made were ones that no listener would ever dare to repeat – even execution would not be enough to dispel the crime.

The year before I began writing this diary, an older man, a railway engineer who had studied in Japan, exposed a man in the small group's lifestyle-examination meeting. The man he exposed was an agricultural technician, a graduate of a vocational school. The engineer accused the technician of saying that Soviet atomic bombs were inferior to those made by the Americans. Surprisingly, the young technician was cool and calm-headed – he stood before the Troop Leader and denied the accusation.

'I never said any such thing!' he said. 'I've only been alive some twenty years and I've never been outside my own province. How could I compare the quality of Soviet bombs to American bombs? I don't even have a clue what an atomic bomb looks like. This is something only a running dog brought up on Japanese imperialism would know. Someone who has experienced all aspects of capitalism all over the world. I may have made mistakes, but my class background is poor peasant.

'Troop Leader, just ask him what class he comes from! Everybody here knows that his father was a capitalist. He's intentionally instilling in all of us here the idea that Soviet atomic bombs are not as good as American atomic bombs! Taking advantage of the lifestyle-examination meeting to put out counter-revolutionary statements!'

The Troop Leader thought this over. Then he said, 'Right! We have here a big intellectual and a small intellectual. The quality of a country's atomic bombs is something only a big intellectual would know. Even leaving aside the question of class background, the little intellectual can still be considered his own man.*

He pointed at the old engineer's nose and yelled at him. 'You dogshitter, are you playing tricks with us? You're worse than just an interpreter for the Japanese devils. Doing labour reform, and you still dare to disseminate counter-revolutionary talk. Didn't you get enough of it outside? Dogshitter! Let's see what Lao-zi wants to do with you today!'

Right then and there, the old engineer was tied up tightly with a rope. He had meant to be the informer, not the one informed on, and he passed out.

At the year-end rewards-and-punishments meeting, he was again made a target for punishment and was marched away to be locked up. To a criminal convict, being sent to a regular labour reform troop seemed like heaven; to the old engineer it was like falling from the seventeenth layer of hell down to the eighteenth. Not long after, we heard that he had stolen a rope and hanged himself in his new troop's horse corral.

'Serves him right!' the technician said to me quietly after this happened. 'I thought he was a human being – I figured he had been overseas, seen a lot, knew a lot. So I talked to him about how I really felt. And he turned out to be less than human. He was just a demon-ghost come to scare and expose people. Sure enough, now he's really a ghost.'

*Not a spy for another country.

Intellectuals who liked to expose other people and write 'small reports' often came up against this kind of thing. Everyone knows that not all the fruit that comes from the same tree is equally sweet.

And so I now exhorted Ma Weixiao: 'Old Ma, what you've just said gets to my ears and no further. Whatever you do, don't let anyone else hear it. And if someone else exposes you in the future, I'll say I don't know a thing. I never heard you say these things.'

He smiled gently. 'Rest easy. I would never drag someone else down with me. A man like me can't be reformed, even over a lifetime. I'll never be like some of them, dogs biting dogs.'

All intellectuals had to take an oath swearing that they would reform themselves completely. Some, in their eagerness, tried to claim that they were already reformed. Ma was unique in announcing that he would never, in his entire lifetime, be reformed. I simply stared at him, so astonished I forgot to breathe.

'You see,' he added proudly, 'there's no way they can force me to go hungry. Even after sending me here to do hard labour, I eat better and have better things than any cadre. Why do I need to beg from them? I can tell them to fart off! I don't ask them for anything so there's nothing they can do. I will never submit to them.'

Later, China's people became poorer and poorer. And the sound of 'Long live Chairman Mao!' did indeed become ever more strident. I began to realize that the teachings espoused by this Muslim were based on a pretty clear understanding of human nature. Some thirty years later, I remember his tale with absolute clarity.

30 August
Farm Sixteen dug sweet potatoes. From what I could see, almost all the men working in the dry fields were stealing things to eat. Zhou Wenlin ate a lot of old *gaochen*, I myself ate sunflower seeds. At noon, Troop Leader Sun and Station Leader Yan called a meeting, originally to discuss productivity; instead they again talked about stealing and escaping. Su Xiaosu, Fan Haoru and a man who had escaped were hauled up to be photographed. After getting home, Fang, Ma and Bai were taken to another meeting of all the small groups.

31 August
Finished work cleaning up Farm Sixteen vegetable fields. Not a man in the entire group wasn't stealing. Sunflower seeds, corn stalks, sweet potatoes, etc. Even Group Leader Heh ate sweet potatoes. Yesterday the leaders harangued on the subject of escapees. Today Fang Aihua escaped and even left a note, saying that Group Leader Heh was trying to get back at him in revenge. Later Fang came back on his own, as though he had taken the day off, outside. When material things are in scarce supply, relations between people become abnormal: they become callous relationships based on naked economic benefit. My mood particularly irritable today, must control it.

*R*eaders under the age of thirty may find the term 'lowered-rations-to-be-substituted-with-gourds-and-greens' rather strange. What could it mean? It looks like a translation of some western culinary trick.

After the buying and marketing of grain became a state monopoly, a new system was put into effect for distributing food. A monthly allocation of grain was made to every person in the country. The amount was rationed and was specific for each person. Adults had an adult portion rationed to them, children had a child's portion. Babies who were still nursing also had a ration, but naturally theirs was given to the mother.*

At the beginning, the allocations were just enough to get by on. By the time of the so-called Three-Years-of-Natural-Disaster** both the supply of grain and the amount rationed to people had gone down. Down to what amount? Each region had a different standard. How much did we convicts get? From 1959 to 1960, the monthly ration for each person dropped from twenty jin to fifteen jin, and then it fell further to nine jin.† The Old Commissar and the Troop Leader were correct when they said that in many places the people, the masses, were not getting as much as the convicts. This reduction of the monthly allocation is what was meant by the term 'lowered rations'.

When I say we were getting nine jin of grain, it should be understood that the grain was unhusked. It had been

*This encouraged women to have more babies.
**Generally indicates late 1959 to late 1962.
†Twenty-two lbs to 16.5 lbs to 9.9 lbs.

ground with skin and husk still on it. Man's intestines have not yet developed to the point that, like ruminants, they can digest husks. When the skin and husk material was eaten, it all got plugged up in the guts. This was what led to that counter-revolutionary saying about being unable to shit after eating steamed buns made of millet.

It was obvious that this grain ration was insufficient to maintain a man's life. What to do? As the Old Commissar said, 'Naturally, Chairman Mao has a way! And what the Old Man has thought of is called "lowered-rations-to-be-substituted-with-gourds-and-greens".

'As the Great Leader taught us, we have to take a planned approach to grain consumption,' the Old Commissar continued. 'He said, "Eat more when you are busy, less when you are not, eat dry food when you have to work hard, wet gruel when you don't. Space the dry and the wet out in sequence, and vary it with things like sweet potatoes and pumpkins." '

This latter was what was known as 'substituting-with-gourds-and-greens'. It was a traditional method used by poverty-stricken peasants in China. China has a saying about eating nothing but chaff and wild plants for half the year. Now the practice was being applied to the New Society throughout the country.

In fact, we convicts did not get anywhere near nine jin of grain. If we had, where would the Old Commissar and Troop Leader have found enough energy to control us? Without eating our food, they would never have had the strength to give all those reports! And what about taking care of the freed convicts who had to be looked after? What about the Big Rats who schemed their way into working in the granary or the kitchen? A single cook could eat the rations of four convicts. No, the 'lowered-rations' part of the phrase was just to make it sound good. What we got was the substitute, the 'gourds-and-greens'.

The food that came out of the kitchen was not very different from the many plants that grew outside, in Nature, so when convicts got to a field it was as though they had jumped out of a tiny rice bowl into a huge food pot. All around them were things to eat. Whatever got pulled up went straight into the mouth. This practice was what was known as 'eating greens'.

What we ate was not limited to green things, to all those jade-green living things around. There were also many small animals on the ground. The problem was catching them. Mice were the most trouble – they could dart off faster than a man could run. Frogs also weren't easy. Although frog-flesh is beautiful and delicious – it's called 'field chicken' in gourmet meals – frogs jump much higher and further than mice. Men near starvation often had to gulp back their saliva and watch as the backs of their quarry leaped away.

The most convenient things were those that jumped only a little and not very far. Things that hunkered on the ground, or crawled along it. These included toads and lizards. Lizards love to stick their tongues out and frighten people but in fact they have no way to combat you. And there were little dead fish, found days after they had died, in dried-up pools of water.

Various works of literature describe the first man to eat an oyster as courageous. There were countless courageous men in the labour reform camps. The scientific name of a toad in Chinese is a *chanchu*. The bodies of some of them can get to be ten centimetres long. Textbooks say that this kind of amphibian is poisonous, that unlike the frog the toad should never be eaten. The dried venom, or 'toad-cake', made from the toad is used in Chinese medicine to treat ulcerous tumours. The reason the medicine has any use is that behind the ears and on the skin of the toad are glands that contain certain substances. Usually the extract is applied as an external potion; if used internally, the medicine should be taken carefully, in extremely small doses. Personal experiments by Chinese in a China that was undergoing a policy of 'lowered rations', however, completely demolished this scientific conclusion.

There are two ways to eat toad: boiled and roasted. There were also convicts who didn't use either of these methods – they would simply gut the toad, skin it, and pop it in their mouths as a cold appetizer. Did somebody say that toads are poisonous? Go to hell! Not only are they not poisonous, the flavour is delicious. Men who dared to eat toad back then are living quite happily today; those who were too squeamish died long ago.

On the 29th, 'Zhou found half a rabbit leg, cooked and ate it.' I remember that everyone was envious of his good fortune, which is why I specifically wrote it into the diary. This half a rabbit leg was left over from the meal of a hawk; it was crawling with maggots and ants. Zhou shook off the ants and picked off the maggots, then held it up to the sunlight to take a look. From nearby I could see its translucent, fresh, pinkish colour. It hadn't gone rotten yet. Zhou was a doctor, so after he appraised his find he said in an excited voice, 'Damn! For better or worse, it's bound to have a gamey flavour! Who's got a match?'

A convict at his side hastily pulled out a match. Whoever produced the match would also get a share – at least he would be given a tiny bite. That was because matches too were rationed.

In stories about the labour reform camps in the Soviet Union and Eastern Europe there are often scenes where a convict pulls out a knife to fight for a small piece of bread. But our race is a meek one. I have done labour reform twice and in all that time I never saw a convict use a knife in order to get something to eat. Where would he get such a weapon? It is clear that the administration of camps in other countries is much more relaxed. Besides, we abhor violence. 'We' being especially the most refined essence of our race, namely intellectuals. We could never hope to beat a criminal convict in a fight anyway, so it was better to be restrained, to use all our energy on experimenting to see what kinds of animals and plants might be edible.

The first person to eat a toad, a rat, a lizard, a dead fish from a dried-out pond, mushrooms that were said to be poisonous – the first to eat *any* of these was an intellectual. Our intellectuals showed themselves to be courageous at least in scientific endeavour. Thieves and rascals would never have this kind of courage: their courage was used to steal ready-made food.

It should not be assumed that these experiments were something wretched, something miserable to watch. In fact, just as in a regular laboratory, they were full of scientific interest. The previous fall, late in 1959, at a time when toads were at their fattest but had not yet begun to hibernate, I ran into one of these courageous types. I had got a slip from the clinic giving me permission to take total rest – permitting me to stay at 'home' and

189

sweep the compound. I went from door to door with a broken old broom sweeping up the dust.

(As I have said before, there was no garbage at all in the camp's large compound. Strangely, three years of natural disaster not only affected agricultural production, but factories too seemed to stop producing, so that there was a shortage of all common articles. Torn fabric, old envelopes, frayed hemp ropes, little bottles, wrapping paper, a small length of cotton thread, and especially cigarette butts, were all regarded as treasures by anyone who found them. Looked at in terms of the lowered rations, even the scabs on one's lips when they split could be considered a kind of meat that was edible. It was hard to consider anything trash, to be thrown out.)

After the convicts had gone to work, the compound of the camp looked very much like that of an old 'mule shed' in north-west China. Mule sheds used to be the only form of hotel in remote areas – it was more important to put up and feed the animals, since humans could sleep anywhere. Although there was no trash in our camp compound, there were cart tracks everywhere, also undried gobs of spit and traces of urine. Every corner reeked of the stench of human livestock.

Just as I was sweeping, I saw a man who had been a historian carrying an enamel pot full of steaming hot water into his barracks. He too was obviously playing at being sick today. He looked excited. Seeing me he sniggered, and gave me a knowing look. So I followed him into the room.

'What would you say this is?' He carefully removed the lid from the pot, then waited for my answer with delight and anticipation.

I looked intently through the rolling steam for a moment, and said without conviction, 'It must be an egg. Where did you ever get an egg?'

'Ha ha!' He laughed happily. 'An egg! Where would I get an egg? Would you please go and buy one for me?' Using chopsticks, he peeled the skin off the puffed-out white belly, then turned the thing over to show its back.

'Ah! It's a frog!'

'Ha ha! Catch a frog for me if you can! It's a toad! Can't you tell?'

I really couldn't tell. The white flesh looked as white as an egg. Only its four little legs were dark. None the less, I stepped backwards in disgust.

'How can you eat that thing? Isn't it poisonous?'

I had only a little bit of grass soup in my stomach, but I felt like indulging in the supremely wasteful act of vomiting.

'You don't understand.' He put the lid of the pot back on, then traced a line in the air with his finger. Although like me he had lost his hair, his two thick, bushy eyebrows made up for it. Under these thick brows were a pair of inviting eyes. He was heavier than I was, and tall. Even now, he had not lost his professional manner. He began his oration:

'Many animals and plants contain a very small amount of poison; almost all Chinese herbal medicaments have some in them. In fact, the effectiveness in treating disease of the herbs, bark, snakes, scorpions and other odd things in Chinese medicine all comes from the part of them that is "poisonous". Nowadays you mention poison and everybody gets scared, but they don't fully comprehend the implications of the concept. They have a twisted idea of what poisonous means. Some poisons not only don't hurt people but actually help clean out toxic elements in the body, kill malignant cells and so on.

'Then there's fire. Fire! Fire is the most powerful weapon man has to subjugate nature, to transform nature. Only after discovering fire and putting it to use was man able to expand the range of what he could eat. He increased his nourishment, leading to an improvement in his physique. Most poisonous elements can be eliminated or modified by the application of fire: by roasting, boiling, steaming, baking.

'Don't look down on the lowly toad. It's true that his outside is ugly and his whole body is covered with tumour-like knobs. And it is indeed written that the toad is poisonous. But it is only poisonous on its skin and in certain glands. You take his skin off and get rid of the glands, heat him up and he turns into perfectly good meat!

'What's more,' he suddenly knitted his brows slightly and the heavy responsibility of being a scientist showed on his face, 'I'm thinking of not taking off the skin and glands. Just boiling it up, to see whether or not it really has any poisonous effect after it's well cooked. Perhaps those poisonous elements are actually beneficial to the human body. After all, isn't the toad included in Chinese medicine? Yes! Perhaps it possesses a very high nutritional value. Coffee was discovered in the fifteenth century when an Ethiopian shepherd cooked it – by now, it's sold all over the world, isn't it?'

Since this man's crime had been mentioned in the papers, virtually all of the intellectuals in the camp knew why he was sent in to do labour reform. He had been a lecturer in the history department of a famous university in the north-west. Before 1957, he maintained that man's earliest history should not be divided simply into Stone Age, Bronze Age and Iron Age as ideology dictated. He felt that there should be a wooden age before the Stone Age. He was convinced that there was a period when man used primarily wooden tools. He collected many myths and legends from the classics to support this thesis, from *Guan zi, Lie zi, Zhuang zi, Huainan zi*, and so on.*

He also cited as evidence the research results of our famous archaeologist, Jia Lanpo. Jia Lanpo had determined from work done on primitive man at Zhoukoudian that the most effective way of hunting at the time was with a wooden club and by burning an entire mountainside to flush out the animals. Like a madman, this lecturer and soon-to-be convict went around advertising his theory. He talked about it in the teachers' room, while delivering lectures, in meetings, after meetings, all the time. He wrote articles about it and sent them to newspapers and magazines. Unfortunately, wooden tools decompose, so he could not find any physical evidence among excavated materials to confirm his idea. The worst thing was that his theory quite obviously did not conform to the *History of Social Development* that the central authorities had said was required reading. It also went against the Educational Programme mandated by the Education Department.

The school warned him repeatedly that he should not use the New-Style-of-University developed by the proletariat to propagate views of the capitalist class. They said he was attempting to disseminate views about history that they described as subjective idealism. Watching

*Chinese Daoist classics.

the fervour with which this intellectual convict argued about the edibility of toads and hearing the unstoppable eloquence with which he put his arguments, I could see that he still suffered from 'addiction to words'. One could imagine that his differences with the authorities of his school had been quite violent.

His dispute with them was not resolved till 1957: 'Using the pretext of research into historical scholarship, madly hoping to overthrow the glorious truth of the development of social history, Professor X went on to deny . . .' – following this came a string of verdicts. Before he even had time to learn to recite them properly as he was supposed to, he was sent to do hard labour.

'Well, what do you think? Try it out! It's a little tougher than frog meat, that's all.' Raising his chopsticks, he generously invited me.

'No! Thank you. Thank you very much.' Although I was extremely hungry I politely declined. From the look of his face, it was clear that he had eaten a lot of toads. He still had plenty of flesh underneath his skin. How else would he have had the strength to deliver such a torrent of words on toads?

I couldn't help but ask him, 'This probably isn't the first time?'

He silently acknowledged with a smile.

Not only was he not poisoned, but thanks to the nutritious value of toad meat he survived in a healthy state all the way until graduation. (Toads could be found for almost eight months out of the year in the fields around the camp, and in the winter you could dig them out of their holes.)

The president of his former university was also a

famous intellectual, who actually invited him back to the university after his graduation from the labour camp. This favourable turn in one's fortunes was highly unusual in the camps. Although his right to give lectures was taken away, he was allowed to copy and write things within the department. But the president's action unintentionally did him a disservice. His addiction to words and his addiction to disputation had not been cured by labour reform. At the least provocation, the problem would erupt again, and universities were precisely the sort of place that induced the disease. As a result, his illness got worse. Six years later, this historian who had espoused the theory that mankind's social development should include a wooden-tools stage died at the hands of the most primitive of wooden cudgels. Those wielding the cudgels were not Neanderthals, however, but a group of Red Guards from one of the best universities in the country.

I admit that I am relatively timid, and this may be because I am a poet and not a scientist. I never participated in his kind of experiment. Even though the historian had proved that toads were edible, I did not eat them.

Trying to eat something that everyone knows you can eat, however, sometimes required a great deal more energy, and also luck. In addition, it meant taking a risk. I am talking about the following experience.

An older convict who was 'being looked after' and I were cutting grass on an uncultivated piece of land. The Main Troop was working in the rice paddies, some distance away. The sun was directly overhead. It was impossible to shield oneself from the heat; the entire world seemed radiant with piercing green rays of light.

The two of us had our backs down and were cutting away, when suddenly a black and white dairy cow came stumbling out of the underbrush.

She stopped when she saw the two of us, and stared at us with wide gentle eyes, as though she were about to ask directions. As she stood there, I saw nothing but the thick udders of milk under her belly. They were round and glistening, firm and completely full. Against the background of green, these udders emitted a mouth-watering milky-white glow.

'Hey! I whispered. 'Get your cup ready.' I cast a look at the old convict. He immediately understood. He dropped his sickle and quickly went to get the enamel cup he used for water. With him on one side and me on the other, we slowly moved to opposite sides of the cow. She looked at us questioningly, one eye seemingly watching each man. I prayed to myself, If you're here on account of God's looking after us pitiful men, then hold still. If I get just one taste of milk, I will thank God for ever. I will become a believer. As we got closer and closer, I became more and more nervous, until we stopped, motionless.

The old convict had been a philosophy scholar at St John's University in Shanghai. This was an utterly useless field of expertise. After coming to the north-west, he had no choice but to teach English in middle school. In 1958, a resounding political slogan was heard throughout China: 'Surpass England in fifteen years and catch up with America!' In its short version, it was 'Pass England catch America.' The old convict wanted to represent himself well, so he wrote a poem on the walls of the school. He gave an artistic twist to the slogan, so that it became

'Surpass heroes catch beautiful women, help Communism get established fast!*

The Secretary General of the Party in the university
was outraged. 'This is not a question of improper use of
words, this is clearly a manifestation of a deep-seated
ideological problem!'

The man was capped** with the hat of 'Americanized
Imperialist' and sent to the camps to do labour reform.

He had been raised on western bread, and naturally
he was also fond of milk. At this moment he was so
excited that his whole body was trembling; the cup in
his hand was shaking up and down as though it was on
springs. He ached to drink some milk, but, standing
there looking at the cow, he just did not know how to
manage it. He stood rooted to the spot like an old tree.
His bald pate, stuffed full of philosophical questions,
was sweating profusely.

Damn! I'd have been better off with one of those petty
thieves! I said to myself. There was nothing for it but for
me to pretend to be harmless and, with a murmur of
reassurance, I moved ever closer to the cow. When I got
right up to her, though, she could probably see the death
mask on my face – especially my eyes, which were
gleaming with avaricious greed. She swivelled around,
tossed up her heels and ran. The shrubs behind blocked
her way, so she turned back, and pounded along the
grassy field.

As soon as she moved to run, my soothing murmur
stopped and my face became a hideous grimace as I

*The characters for 'England' mean 'heroic country' in Chinese; the
characters for 'America' mean 'beautiful country'.
**Accused of committing a counter-revolutionary crime.

leaped in her direction. The open plain then became the arena for a Spanish bullfight, as a battle ensued between man and beast. The philosopher seemed to be still at his lectern – without moving his feet, he spread his arms and shouted, moving to face her as she circled around. It was impossible for me to catch her by myself – in the end, she got away.

As she moved into the distance, her fat udders swung back and forth. When she was far enough to feel safe, she stopped on top of a small hill and actually turned her head around to us as though to snicker. Hee hee, she taunted, come and catch me if you can! Come on! Try it again!

But we were too exhausted to move. We bent over, hands on knees, and gasped and coughed. I silently decided that from this day onward I would never believe in God. Far away, the teats glistened as though they were about to burst with milk. They were supernaturally beautiful in the bright sunshine. Thinking of what had happened, the two of us couldn't help laughing. Once started we couldn't stop, and from a chuckle we soon went to roaring laughter. Then, from the laughter we went to wild sobbing. 'Ha ha ha ha ha hnn hnn hnn hnn . . .' Unable to stand up, we fell, laughing and crying, to the ground.

After a while, the sound of our voices stopped suddenly, together. I remember discovering that the tears rolling down my face tasted astringent. Like the laughter, the bitter, sour tears could not be held back – they silently flowed down my thin sharp cheeks and dripped on to the green ground.

The soil of China has an abundance of water at its disposal.

I later dreamed often of those two full udders. From then on, if I ever saw a woman with good-looking breasts, they made me think first of eating, not of sex. It's still that way today.

'My mood particularly irritable today, must control it.' Under the circumstances, it is surprising that I was still making demands on myself in the area of self-refinement. I didn't know if the world and life were basically like what I was experiencing, or if I had somehow moved outside the bounds of normality. Everything I saw around me was different from what I had read in books. The humanistic Man eulogized by poets, authors, scholars of ethics, educators, philosophers, historians, seemed to have been reduced to a state that made him not very different from the toads he was eating. All animals on the globe, even at the lowest level, seemed to conform to the natural laws of their own beings. There was nothing incomprehensible about that. It was just hard to understand why man should be leading this kind of life.

In fact, I had no wish to understand. I just lived on, morning to night, with a kind of unspeakable wonder at what was happening. That I kept on living, still not wanting to die, and still even placing demands on myself to be a better person – that was truly something to wonder at.

Take 30 August, for example. On that day, a convict was declared an escapee by Troop Leader Sun and Station Leader Yan. On the 31st, his body was found in a corn field by a freed convict who was driving a cart.

It turned out he had not tried to escape, but instead had died of bloating up. The way he died is something an ordinary person cannot understand. Corn is just beginning to ripen in August. While out working, this fellow had slipped into the corn field when no one was looking. He ripped off an earful of corn and ate it, ripped off another and ate it, until he had eaten over twenty ears of not fully ripened corn.

When the freed convict hauled the body back into camp, its convict shirt and pants were in shreds – they were like the skin of a toad that has been burst open by a swollen belly. The belly itself had not cracked open, but the swollen corpse filled the entire back of the cart. The free convict, who came from the peasant class, wanted to put it on display in the threshing ground. Before he could do it, the Troop Leader came and cursed him.

'What kind of talk is that? You want a demonstration? No point – one dead of his kind, one fewer. Don't even unload him. Tomorrow take him straight out to the graveyard and bury him.'

Getting food that evening, I talked to this freed convict at the window of the big kitchen. 'Smelly!' he said. 'It stank so much don't even mention it. If you eat raw corn it begins to ferment in your belly. Of course it swells up! The idiot didn't even know that simple truth. And he was supposed to be someone who's read books!

'How do I know he ate over twenty ears of corn? Because I picked up twenty-odd corncobs along the road. The bastard had gnawed every one clean of every single kernel.

'No, he had no intention of escaping. From where he started pulling off the corn to where the bastard collapsed was on the way back to camp, the direction going home. For sure he walked that far and his stomach began to swell. So he couldn't go any further. Just before dying he must have hurt like hell because the entire area of corn stalks had been broken down where he rolled around . . .'

This peasant-class freed convict knew that you can't eat uncooked corn, that at the very least you can't eat a lot of it, whereas the well-read intellectual lacked this basic knowledge. The man had once been in the same group with me, and we had some contact. He too was very young; he had been a primary-school teacher in the city. His mother died early and his father pulled a rickshaw in the Old Society. The father had suffered and yet done all he could to pull his son up in life, serving both as mother and father and providing an education so that the son could eventually graduate from a teachers' college.

Why was he doing labour reform? He never dared to tell anyone. If you asked him, he would shake his head with acute distress: 'I can't tell you! I can't tell you! If I said anything, it would be disseminating counter-revolutionary statements.'

He often came to work with a tattered copy of a dictionary tucked under his arm. Knowing that I liked to read, he told me to follow his own example. 'Don't read anything else! Just a dictionary – it's the safest. Nobody can say that this book has any political problems. In any event, when you have only a few spare moments, it doesn't matter where you start or get to if you're reading a dictionary.'

A valuable lesson! Since a dictionary has no plot, and lacks any sense of reader involvement, it cannot be so engaging that you are unwilling to put it down. There was still enough food to go around at that time, and criminal convicts often told dirty jokes to the intellectuals. Seeing him reading all day, silent and absorbed, they would joke that he was thinking of women. One time, he said to me in an aggrieved way, 'I wasn't thinking of women. I was thinking of my father. How much I owe him and how sorry I am. Oh well, they can say I'm thinking whatever they wish.' And he went back to his dictionary.

Under the entry for corn, though, the dictionary did not say that one cannot eat too much if it isn't cooked. He must have been quite amazed that he died.

His face was clean-cut and intelligent, with a high, wide brow. His deep-set eyes flashed with a seldom-seen honesty. As a result, when they saw that he had not returned from work that day, the Troop Leader and Station Leader were particularly angry that this man, of all men, had escaped.

'Damn him! You expect some of them to try to escape. But they're still around, while here's one you would never have thought of and he's gone! After him! We've got to bring this one back and do a thorough denunciation.'

One of the first things you have to know if you want to survive in our society is: you must preserve consistency in the impression you give to the leaders. If the leaders have always thought of you as being all right, but you do something unexpected that they don't like, then you will be punished many times beyond what is normal.

On the other hand, if the leaders consider you a bad egg from the start, and you do bad things, they will often forgive you. You have to start with the premise that you are 'your own man'. 'That dogshitter!' they will say. 'Damn it all, if he doesn't get up to this kind of despicable thing, who's going to do it?! Ha ha!' And they have a good laugh about it.

I had a dream the night after we heard about this young man's death. In the dream, all I could see were his two honest eyes looking questioningly at me. The background was indistinct. Could it have been that stretch of corn field? This is something I did not record in the diary – instead, I told myself to be less irritable. To this day, I find that amazing.

I have long since forgotten why I was irritable on that day, and what expression my irritability took. But I can guarantee that it had something to do with eating. I also know that the entry contained some clues – a code for another meaning. By now I can't tell you what it was, nor, for the sake of these notes, can I fabricate something. There isn't much need to fabricate anything anyway, since everything in that life was more moving than a made-up story.

For example, in the entries I mention a man named Su Xiaosu. Su was hauled before the Troop to 'have his picture taken', all because he had picked up an ear of corn on the road to work. This ear of corn may have been dropped by neighbouring farmers who came into our fields to steal in the middle of the night; Su Xiaosu picked it up, shucked it and ate it.

Unlike Zhou, who found the rabbit leg, Su did not have the good fortune to come upon this ear of corn in private. The Troop Leader saw him pick it up and promptly ordered him to throw it down. He couldn't bear to do that, however – he refused to let it go. Instead, he fiercely gnawed at it without stopping. Indeed, he gnawed faster and faster, so that white spit foamed at the sides of his mouth.

This made the Troop Leader furious. He lifted his rope and lashed down at him with it. The Troop Leader's skill with the rope was like that of a circus performer – each lash of the rope was placed smack on the hands holding the ear of corn. Not a single whiplash met empty air. He kept it up until Su Xiaosu's hands were covered with blood, until he was madly devouring his own blood with the corn. Still Su did not let go, would not stop. Heart and soul he gnawed, gnawed, gnawed. It was as though he had no feeling of pain. When he finished the corn, he threw away the cob, then used his tongue to lick clean every corner of his mouth, inside and outside. He paid no attention to the blood flowing from his wounds, so that the road was covered with spatters of red.

After work, he was dragged before the troop to be photographed. A crust of blood already covered the wounds on his hands, and he seemed to have even less sensation than before. The Troop Leader and the Station Leader cursed him, and he just gazed this way and that, looking very self-satisfied to have been able to eat an ear of corn.

It should be noted here what a 'photograph' involved. The word was another way of saying a Public Exhibition, which was the technical term used for criminal punishments. Naturally I refer to the ancient form of criminal punishments, not our advanced modern methods. In the old days, China had such punishments as putting a cangue on a man and then publicly exhibiting him, or putting him in a tiny wooden cage and exhibiting him. We Chinese have taken these as our inheritance, and have carried them a step further.

In 1958, when we were still able to get enough to eat,

the leaders of the labour reform camps would rack their brains to think up various poses and ways to parade us convicts around – to have us 'photographed' when we had offended the rules. One way was to tie a man securely to a carrying pole, then, with his head down and his feet up, place him on an incline of about seventy-five degrees. The person was generally set upside-down on the side of the big canal. This was known as 'letting the blood trickle down', and was the most common form of punishment.

Another was to take off a man's upper clothes and tie him to a tree to let the insects and mosquitoes bite him. It is said that this was a method of dealing with deserters in the old warlord armies. Nowadays, readers might think this a light punishment – a few insect bites should be nothing more than a surface discomfort. Little do they know the mosquitoes in the marshy areas where we were working. A cloud of mosquitoes could not be described as a cloud – the local people generally referred to them quite appropriately as balls.

'Mosquitoes are worked up into a ball! Quick! Run! Huge balls of mosquitoes on the way!' A cloud differs from a ball in that a cloud still has spaces in between insects. A ball is one solid mass. Where we worked, mosquitoes would congregate in the air like morning mist, then attack like bullets, humming on the way.

Convicts who had been KMT soldiers educated me in how to deal with this. Whatever you did, you did not want to wave them away. The best thing was to let them bite you. One soldier they knew who was being punished in this way was accompanied by his friends. The friends couldn't stand to see him suffer, so they sat near by waving as hard as they could. In the end, the man died of mosquito bites.

'When a mosquito has eaten its fill, it can't move,' they told me. 'If you don't shake, your entire body will eventually become covered with a kind of shield of full mosquitoes. Other mosquitoes who want to suck your blood can't get in. As soon as you chase off those who have drunk as much as they can, you make way for new ones who are empty and hungry. That way, delegation after delegation of mosquitoes has a chance at your blood . . . and how much blood do you have to give them?'

These methods of punishment belonged to the sort known as 'still photography'. When the beets were strung around my neck and I got paraded around, that was known as 'action photography'. The most common pose in action photography was to tie a man's hands together and have other convicts pull him along the ground. This was called 'dragging along a dead dog', and it was used specifically on convicts who were unwilling to go to work. The road from the barracks to the working fields was a crude dirt road, crossed by ditches, stubble, brush. By the time he had been dragged all the way to work, one can imagine what a dead dog looked like. He would be left lying beside the field, for everyone to 'photograph'.

Most of the men who were distinguished by being photographed were criminal convicts. Intellectuals might sell out their friends, might tempt other people into saying counter-revolutionary statements and then tell on them, and so on, but when they saw someone being photographed they would start to tremble. And when they themselves were to be photographed? You can imagine.

It's odd, but I felt both sympathy and great respect whenever I saw someone being photographed. I felt that here was one man facing the entire world alone. It was less a matter of everyone else photographing him than it was of his taking a portrait of the world.

When they instituted the 'lowered-rations-to-be-substituted-with-gourds-and-greens' policy, however, cruel methods of punishment no longer really worked. Before the film was even exposed to light, so to speak, the man would die. Nowadays taking a picture of a man was more like regular photography: he would stand in front of the troop and everyone else would use their eyes on him like cameras. That was about it. So after Su Xiaosu was photographed, he happily returned to his home along with everyone else.

Which all just goes to say that, during the period of lowered rations, everything came down to a lowered standard.

1 September

Today considered a rest day, busy as soon as I got up, in fact nothing much happened, but the compound very tense. <u>Life itself is poverty-stricken, devoid of content, leading to poverty-of-thinking syndrome. Every day tasteless labour, turning people's spirit into something more and more base.</u> As soon as they got up, Heh and Zhou cooked up some grass, put in the hot pepper the group had given them, and ate it. After breakfast divided up gourds, each person got 1 jiao 8 fen worth. Afternoon, collective examination of bodies at the clinic. All it meant was weighing and measuring height. Evening the Troop Leader talked about hygiene problems when he called rollcall.

2 September

Morning thinned sweet potatoes Farm Twelve canal. Energy much reduced, every man eating sweet potatoes, sunflower seeds, etc. Troop Leader Zheng called meeting, shouted about eating-greens behaviour. Afternoon picked up bags and transported sweet potatoes. Group Leader Heh said. 'To hell with them. Pointless not to eat – you get nothing out of not eating,' as he madly gnawed a sweet potato. Divvied out 1 jiao worth of sawdust tobacco to Zhu Zhenbang, just a few pinches. Evening studied, struggled against Liu Guangfu.

3 September

Morning dried hemp at Farm Sixteen, then went to vegetable field to transport sweet potatoes. Entire group continued to eat greens. To save face, also because he was afraid Liu Xiangru would report, Heh had to get angry at lunch and ordered everyone to hand over their sunflower seeds. This little scene did not end well, for in the afternoon everybody ate even more on the sly. Zhou and Bai brazenly went to steal watermelon. Heh furious but could do nothing – he slept that night on the edge of the field.

4 September

Cut green fertilizer at Farm Nine canal. Completely exhausted at start of work in morning: Heh also lagged behind. Troop Leader Zheng got angry. Entire group ordered to work an additional hour. According to Liu Xiangru the supply situation in town even worse. Each person three packs of cigarettes a month, and you have to have neighbours certify that you smoke. Took a sweet potato today, gave it to Ding Haiji, made him very happy. Now a sweet potato considered good. Evening, camp leader reported on Double-Counter problems; during discussion Troop Leader Zheng also gave a speech. Gave Ma Weixiao half a jin of grain coupons for guest eater.

The two places that are underlined on 31 August and 1 September are parts of the diary that the investigator who confiscated it in 1970 considered questionable. He drew a wavy line with a blue-coloured pencil under these characters – the rising and falling of the line gives me a queasy feeling. To this day I don't know why these sentences raised doubts, why the investigators should have paid particular attention to them. Was it that they felt that life was *not* 'grim' but warm and wonderful? That it was not vulgar but lofty and noble? That it was not insipid but actually full of excitement? Did they think that since I felt it was grim, vulgar and insipid, this proved that my political thinking was counter-revolutionary?

The saying 'Class struggle must be espoused every day' not only divided people who were basically the same into opposing camps, it also erected high walls inside the mind of each individual. It is not easy for people to understand one another to begin with. When they've been split into 'class camps' it's even more difficult. Not only are you unable to comprehend another camp's thinking, you can't even really connect with people who are supposed to be in your own camp. There might be a few small holes in the high walls, but these turn out to be just for spying through, or shooting out from.

I never knew which words people might find fault with, which sentences might be given counter-revolutionary significance. I still don't know, and as a result even now I am constantly afraid. In this life, this world,

I am floating up and down at the whim of those wavy blue lines.

There are still many alchemists of the Chinese language living quite healthy lives in China today. These people are excellent at finding elements in what I've written that would be quite sufficient to send me in for a third stint of labour reform, even now. If the elements they found were not considered sufficient, they wouldn't hesitate to add a few catalysts, something to make my words produce a 'double reaction', to make them into a different chemical compound altogether.

Actually, the underlined sentences, floating on the blue waves, simply expressed my naïvety. They showed, quite obviously, that I had experienced over seven hundred days of labour reform yet had not even begun to settle into the role of a labour reform convict. I was still expecting life to be rich and colourful; I was still complaining that it was 'devoid of content, leading to poverty-of-thinking syndrome'. I seem to have thought that a labour reform camp should be some kind of university.

I have written 'poverty-of-thinking', but the one thing our impoverished country did not lack at all just then was 'thinking'. The leaders were madly checking out every person's thoughts, sorry only that they could not reach into each brain, scrape out what was there and examine it under a microscope. Every evening, in the small-group discussion meetings, the lifestyle-investigation meetings, during the Individual Thought reports, the Personal Summary of Reform Improvement reports, it was emphasized over and over again that every person had to 'hand over', expose, his own thinking.

'Talk it all out. Say it! Tell us: what have you been thinking recently?'

Leaders would spend enormous time and effort on this – often they would come all the way to the convict's 'home' in the evenings. They would sit there beside the kang, with legs crossed, smiling a little, and they would tempt someone into spilling everything in his head. After Su Xiaosu gnawed the ear of corn and got whipped for it, he was told to 'hand over his thinking'.

'Why didn't you toss away that ear of corn?' they asked. 'The Troop Leader ordered you to get rid of it, and you still kept on! What kind of *thinking* is that?'

What kind of thinking? You certainly could not admit that it was because you were hungry. Hunger was merely a feeling. It wasn't thinking.

'Others eat the same rations as you,' they continued. 'Why aren't you like other people? You did it simply because you want to blacken the name of socialism!'

Peasants did not understand a socialism that told people to endure famine. They were even less able to understand what socialist slogans and imagery had to do with gnawing on an ear of corn. They would blink their tiny eyes furiously as they begged for mercy. 'I'll work harder from now on, from now on I'll work much harder . . .!'

When courageous intellectuals ate toads, lizards and poisonous mushrooms to try to stay alive, the accusation was always: 'They haven't adequately reformed, due to *capitalist thinking!*' It was because they had been 'dominated by capitalist thinking' that such men went out and ate those things.

And if you didn't analyse the problem properly, in this way, then the faces of the leaders immediately lost their smiles. You just wait! The next one to have to 'hand over his thinking' will be you!

'Just look at that! Still wanting to eat meat, even in these times!' An intellectual had been discovered just as he was stewing up a rat to eat. The Group Leader carried out his pot, blackened with soot from the fire, to make a 'report', that is to expose him. After being told about it, the Old Commissar immediately called the convicts together for a meeting. Lifting the pot up high, he exhibited the rat meat as he lectured us.

'Maybe you all don't realize! Right now, even Chairman Mao is not eating meat. He's going through hard times right along with the rest of us. But this lousy rightist element has no self-awareness! He's still trying to think of any way he can to eat some meat. Are you ashamed of yourself or are you not! Let's everyone give him a struggle session, denounce him for his *capitalist-class self-indulgent thinking*!'

The rat meat was poured out; the blackened pot was also confiscated. Everybody stared hard at this rightist who liked to eat meat. He sat in the midst of us, hanging his head. I saw tears shining from his eyes. But I didn't know if he was longing for the rat meat that had been almost ready to eat, or whether, moved by the Great Leader's example, he was ashamed of himself.

After one's thinking had been 'revealed' in such encounters over the course of several weeks, we would have what was referred to as the Thought Line-up.

The Thought Line-up, mentioned in the entry for 29 August in the diary, would be carried out every month or every two months. Those sent to the end of the line after this process were those who had the worst thinking. It is worth mentioning Ma Weixiao here, the Muslim who told me that he was someone who would 'never ever be properly reformed'.

Ma played the important role of arbiter in the small group during these sessions. He would say very little while people were debating. He would sit there leaning against his bedding, stroking his three lovely tufts of beard. Debates would go on endlessly in the course of getting a proper line-up – don't think that people who were dying of hunger lacked interest in it. Even criminal convicts didn't want to get left behind. Was this because if someone ended up last in the line every time he'd be punished? Not necessarily. Those who were arrested for crimes and elevated into the ranks of a regular labour reform camp were not the 'backward elements' who always came at the end of the Thought Line-up. They were men who had committed some physical crime. To be put in the front ranks of the line-up all the time also didn't guarantee that you would be graduated ahead of time.

Men were intensely interested because in this debate about 'thinking' we had one of our few chances to express ourselves as human beings – we had lost most other necessary conditions for being called human. Here we could persuade ourselves that we were not cows, horses, toads, lizards or something else. Only in this tiny arena could a man gain a modicum of psychological comfort. So we fought to establish our own dignity, our right to the title 'man', on this palm-sized bit of space – a realm called 'thought' that the leaders, out of charity, had bestowed on us.

By rights, Ma Weixiao should have placed first in the Thought Line-up: he didn't eat greens, he didn't trade and he wasn't lazy when it came to work. He modestly put himself in second place every time though – in this way he gained credibility and the right to judge the thinking of everyone else. When the small-group meeting was about to conclude, when everyone had talked enough and was ready to pull down his bedding and go to sleep, the Group Leader would finally ask his opinion.

'What about it?' he would say. 'Old Ma, what do you think?'

Old Ma would lower the hand with which he had been stroking his beard. His eyelids would slowly close as he concentrated. Finally, in a serious tone, he would begin. 'I think . . . how about this. One, two, three, four . . .'

He would always line us up in just the right way. The outsider is always the one who sees things most clearly, but then too it took someone who was getting enough to eat to be so astute. He would never allow someone to place last every time – even if a man's representation of himself was always bad. The last name had to be changed often.

The Group Leader, on the other hand, always had to be number one, whether his 'self-representation', his behaviour, had been good or bad. Old Ma made manifest the philosophy regarding 'good' that he had described to me. And, indeed, not a single person did not submit to him, did not consider him good.

Thanks to his thoughtfulness, I was always placed just about in the middle. Slightly towards the back, not the front. So far as I can remember, he never put me at the beginning, even though I was the record keeper of the small group, its Secretary General.

'You!' he said from behind me. 'What's all this! You've got up to all kinds of trouble: eating greens, trading things, even escaping! Your work is also sloppy and lazy. It goes without saying you can't be put before others.

You even pulled up good sprouts instead of bad ones. Despite all that, the leaders often look after you. How do you think others take that? You go last!'

I gulped. I had considered my thinking, that is my political consciousness, not too bad.

Later he ridiculed me in private. 'What use is good thinking? Who cares! Child, the greatest good is to be alive. First make sure your own life is preserved, *then* think about everything else. As they say, leave a little greenery on the mountain and you won't have to worry about firewood in the future.'

I believe that I represent a rather special kind of intellectual. In terms of 'thinking' I consider myself pretty uncommon. The wings of my spirit roam above the vulgar, practical world. In terms of behaviour, though, I stick stubbornly to the rules of survival. If it contributes to staying alive, there is nothing that I won't do.

For example, on 31 August I have written that Fang Aihua escaped and then came back. In fact, I was the cause of his escape. When Ma Weixiao said I had escaped, he meant not only that time I ran away for fifteen days, but also once before then, when I briefly took off. He mentioned it because my short tour of sightseeing had a great impact on what happened later at the camp – its ramifications went beyond the escapes of criminal convicts, who would jump the wall and never look back.

After I set that precedent, people started escaping from the camp in droves. They would leave for just a day, then come back to write a self-examination and be penitent. Some would even write the self-examination before they left. Fang Aihua's invention was that instead of writing a self-examination he wrote an explanation of why he had escaped. Because of this, the one who got all hell from the leaders after he had escaped and returned was not him but the Group Leader.

From the above, the reader will note that in some respects the way the camps and the way society at large controlled people was roughly the same. There was no control in the sense of watch-guards or even a legal system. Yet discipline was strictly enforced. The inadequacies of the laws and the guards both in the camps and Outside were more than made up for by a tight system of thought control.

In the camps, every small group had an appointed Group Leader, who functioned like the head of a family. As in the old manor-house system, with peasants dependent on the house and vice-versa, people were tied together in an upper- and a lower-class relationship. These ties among people related to all administrative matters, all life-governing matters, which made them tighter than those of simple blood relations.

Each person kept surveillance over the others. No one had better even dream of stepping outside the system. One could hardly think a subversive thought without being found out – the constant political movements inflicted on people in those days made the practice of 'combing through your thinking' a common occurrence. Like fleas or lice, bad thoughts had to be washed out.

And yet, since the thing controlling you depended not on guns but rather on the thoughts inside your own head, if by chance or even intentionally you broke through the thought control it was actually quite easy to leave camp.

Roughly one year earlier, when large numbers of men had begun to die in the camps, I had already become painfully aware of how likely it was that I would starve to death. One day, when the rest of the small group took off for work, I stayed lying there on the kang. There was no real reason for it, although I didn't feel well. I'm not sure why, but nobody noticed, nobody called me or forced me to get up. It was as though the birds had all flown and a wide stretch of forest was now peaceful and soundless. For a brief moment I was anxious: should I chase after the Main Work Troop or should I continue to lie here without moving?

I raised my head and looked around. There was nothing to see but the rumpled bedding of the convicts. In the bright sunlight, the miserable barracks seemed even more ghastly. For the first time, I realized that a so-called home had to have people in it, people doing things, even though they might be no more than petty thieves moving around stealing things. The empty barracks was a microcosm of hell. The meanness of it was all too apparent. If hell has a stench to it, it has to be the damp acrid stink that I was smelling now. Afraid, I crawled out of bed. As I did, I tucked the extra pants that I used for a pillow under my arm. Then I simply marched out of the door.

I walked straight ahead in a daze. As I went through the main gate, I was almost unconscious that I was leaving the compound of the camp. I walked past the bounds of the labour reform camp. With the pants hugged to my chest, I was now walking through the fields of the local people.

This was freedom. I was actually free! Nobody stopped me. Although I ran into a number of labour-reform-camp cadres and workers, also one security man with a gun strapped to his belt, they couldn't imagine that a convict would choose this most public and open means of escape. Here was a man striding along, hugging a pair of cotton trousers – he couldn't be escaping unless he was completely crazy!

It was unpremeditated. I had no plan. I just wanted to throw off the mind control and be free. So simple. But until then nobody had realized just how easy it was.

Carefree and liberated, I walked through the local fields. In the fresh air my mind cleared somewhat, but my first sensation was that I was hungry. Since I was free, I had better put this freedom to good use.

Not far ahead of me was a thatched hut beside a field, for keeping watch over a crop of melons. My liberated feet naturally strode in the direction of food. An old peasant woman was sitting inside, stitching fabric soles for shoes. She was not at all surprised to see me. She even laughed when she saw my pants. The locals around the camps had already learned to treat convicts as though they were neighbours – there was a warm familiarity between us.

'Child, what are you up to?' the old woman said, before I even opened my mouth. 'What's that in your arms? Let me see.'

I handed her the cotton trousers. Then I stretched my neck out and took a good look around her straw shack. She turned out to be even poorer than us convicts. Other than some unripe melons, I could see absolutely nothing with which to appease my hunger. The old woman turned my pants over and over, scrutinizing the seams. Then she turned them inside-out, saying all the while that this machine stitching was not half so good as pants made by hand. In the end, after thoroughly appraising them, she said:

'Want to trade these pants?'

I asked her what she had. Her lips pursed in the direction of the field.

'Watermelon,' she said.

I said they weren't ripe yet.

'Such a big field!' she laughed. 'You think there's no ripe ones? I'll help you choose. I'll fill you full to bursting!'

Blotchy old-age spots showed through the sparse white hair on her scalp. They looked like clouds against an empty sky. Her blue shirt had been patched and the patches had patches on them – it had become like a kind of lined jacket. When she wore them, my brand-new cotton pants would make her old age and bleak situation even more apparent. Still, she spoke brightly and cheerfully. 'Fill you full to bursting' was a local phrase meant to express affection – what she meant was that she would get the best and ripest for me, so many that my stomach would burst if I ate them all.

Her determination to make me burst moved me so much that I choked up with emotion. Well, if it was to be watermelon, let it be watermelon. It was fitting that what was worn in the winter could be traded for something to eat in the summer. No matter what I traded the pants for, it was still a bargain. I might not be alive next winter.

I was incapable of selecting ripe watermelon, however. I held out my useless hands and said I had no idea how to distinguish between what was too green and what was ripe. All I could do was eat them.

She smiled as she looked me up and down. 'Why are you doing labour reform?'

Sent in for writing a poem, I thought to myself. Instead

219

of saying this out loud, which could only make this country woman doubt my truthfulness, I simply pointed to my head. I said that there were problems there.

She sympathized even as she ridiculed me. 'Child, your head is what did you in!'

How true. My head is what did me in. Later, whenever I wanted to use my brain, I would think: Can it be that my head is going to harm me again? This practice continued until it became a habit. The minute I begin to think seriously about something, my heart starts to pound.

She did indeed find a number of ripe melons. She crawled around in the field, and when she straightened up I saw that her face was covered with sweat. Panting, she lifted her shirt to wipe it off, revealing two thin dried-out breasts.

I quickly shouted to her, 'Enough! Enough! I can't eat that many. Please don't pick any more! Come and rest!'

Instead, she let out a long sigh. 'Ai! It's just a shame there's nothing else to give you. Anyway, watermelon. Can't hurt you. Just open up your stomach and eat as much as you can.'

A pile of watermelons was finally set before me. Round and jade-green, they looked absolutely adorable. If I ate them there beside the field, though, and if members of the local commune saw me, they would investigate her. If I carried them back to the barracks the labour reform convicts would see me and investigate me. So the old woman pulled a tattered hemp bag out of her shed, and helped me stuff a few of the watermelons inside. The two of us, me heaving the bag on my back, she supporting from behind, carried them to a small thicket nearby where I would be hidden from sight. It took many trips to transfer them all.

Then she patted my rump, pulled my shirt down for me and said, 'There, child. You just rest here awhile. Eat easy. I'll be off.'

And so I sat down, peaceful and enjoying myself. I began to 'eat easy'.

I would eat for a while, then rest for a while, eat a while longer, then rest for a while. Sometimes I ate sitting, sometimes lying down. Other times I would eat while taking a pee. I ate all the way from noon to dusk, until I had eaten the equivalent of several hemp bags full of watermelon. I would rather have burst my stomach than leave a single melon behind. If a rind had so much as one bite left on it, I would be reluctant to let it go – I'd pick it up again and finish it off.

The old woman had been right: watermelon can't hurt a man. All around me were watermelon rinds and urine. Green-headed ants swarmed everywhere. I rubbed my extended stomach without the slightest feeling of discomfort, still 'eating easy' as I lay in the shade of the trees. When I first started eating I couldn't even taste the flavour of watermelon. After I had had a few I finally realized that the melons were sweet. Then, after eating more, I lost the flavour again – the watermelon juice turned into something like plain water. Now, after resting a long time, when I looked at a white rind and thought back to its pink flesh the sweetness came back to my mouth like fire. I knew then that the most beautiful thing on earth is not discovering the truth, as books say, or sex with a woman, as the criminal convicts were always saying. Instead, the most beautiful thing is to be full.

None the less, after eating, thinking commenced once

again. It seems that filling the stomach and filling the mind come together. The sun was just about to fall behind the mountains. The ants had settled like immobile dust on the ground. Mosquitoes had come out and were beginning to hum. They were uninterested in the watermelon rinds, but they now attacked my arms and covered my face. I could grab a whole fistful just by reaching out a hand to the sky. If I stayed there stretched out on the ground, I would die from mosquito bites, like that photographed convict.

I climbed up, but for a moment was uncertain which way to go. My 'thoughts' told me that I should return to the labour reform camp. After all the study sessions, my thoughts were on such an elevated level that they refused to let me think it was wrong to send me in to do hard labour. I could only think that my unwillingness to do labour reform was wrong.

And so I went back along the road I had come on, stopping at every tree to pee a little, like a dog. I peed all the way back to the labour reform camp.

The Main Work Troop had still not returned from work when I got home, the watermelon I had eaten had not yet been completely digested. So I again lay down on my bedding. What should I do? My thoughts informed me that I should write a self-examination. Lubricated by the watermelon in my stomach, my attitude towards the barracks had changed – it now seemed a kind of heaven rather than hell. Words miraculously flowed from my pen, as I wrote a very detailed and literary self-examination. Every sentence was beautifully, roundly finished, not like the crude notes of most self-examinations. By the time the Main Work Troop returned, my critique was finished. Passing over the Group Leader, I handed it directly to the Troop Leader.

The Troop Leader stood in the compound and read it. A good piece of writing will draw someone in from the start – he read it with relish, then asked, with some curiosity. 'You dogshitter, you're not bluffing me, are you? How can one man eat several bags full of watermelon in one day? Tell me honestly, what mischief were you really up to out there?'

Fortunately the patch of underbush where I had eaten the melons was not too far from the camp. The Troop Leader got his torch and accompanied me to the scene. When he flashed his light around and came upon watermelon rinds everywhere, he couldn't help laughing as he said, 'You dogshitter, you did it! You actually did it!' He had a look of considerable respect on his face.

Sometimes our leaders can be quite likeable. If you show them something interesting, make them happy for a while, they forgive you even if you've gone against the rules. What happened that day became a rehearsal for the next time I escaped. Since I was not punished for it, convicts often began to escape for a day. They would go to the locals, go 'door to door', and then come back again.

The people around were quite willing to receive these convicts who were out for a spin. They loved hearing their stories. Whatever was written down was supposed to serve the needs of politics, and as a result there were nothing but grim newspaper editorials for entertainment. Let there be a tiny bit of some candy or some vegetables to eat and those convicts could talk up their crimes as though heaven were raining flowers. Their exaggerations were both funny and acute. The local people would enjoy hearing a tale and could also get a bargain trading a few things. Why shouldn't they be happy?

From that time, however, I never ate watermelon again. As soon as I tried, my stomach would start to hurt.

5 September

Morning cut grass at large branch canal. Set up a united group, Chen Lin made Group Leader. Yesterday evening had a nightmare, dreamed I was hitting Mama with a shoe. On reflection, perhaps my life here is giving her the same kind of torment. Talked over reform of intellectuals with Chen Lin while cutting grass, ached to express what's inside. Yelled at again by Troop Leader Zheng for eating sunflower seeds. Entire group severely reprimanded, given photograph treatment on side of canal, was last to get any food. Afternoon measured out land – measured all afternoon with Liu Yacheng. Just at time to stop work Troop Leader Zheng announced our crime, including me with the worst offenders at eating greens. Why? I don't understand. Evening suddenly showed movies: National Agricultural Exhibition, National Industrial Commodities Exchange Exhibition and *Red Seeds*. After watching, felt our lives very narrow and limited in comparison to the lives of free citizens. Received letter from Mama. She says no chance of getting flannel pants, plus she doesn't want me to be graduated right now.

6 September

Morning cut grass at Canal One. Did not want to go in water at first, but to maintain face of everyone I went in. Asked Ma Weixiao on my behalf to bring guest food (two steamed millet buns), Zhang Zhiqing and Fang Xuechang escaped to local villagers' fields to steal corn.

7 September

Still cutting green grass, did not go into water. Afternoon measured, met a villager fishing, spent 2 jiao to buy twelve small fish. He cooked them, the two of us split and ate them. Evening at the study session denunciation of material (I was judged a backward element).

8 September

Felt bad soon as I got up, headache, chest hurt. Transported sugar beets at Farm Sixteen, carried less on my back than others at times, was found out by Chen Lin, got criticized. Chen reported it to Troop Leader Zheng. Zheng yelled at me for still putting it on. Afternoon tied hemp in bundles. Some did it sitting, some kneeling – everyone good at turning hard labour into easier labour. Liu Xueru's son came to see him, said in the communes in Hebei people get a ration of only three jin of grain a month. They go to work at three o'clock in the morning, come back at seven o'clock at night. Strange! How can their bodies keep going?

Outrageous or frightening behaviour is generally considered to be the result of a person's losing the ability to reason. Truly unthinkable, terrifying behaviour comes not from a loss of reason, however, but from loss of the ability to feel emotion. Reason can restrain man, guide his behaviour into normal channels. But emotion is the link, the tie that binds people. A man must have normal feelings to maintain ties with the people around him, and only through those ties can a society preserve its normality. When a man feels a measure of love for this world, his reason and intellect can be put to good use. The moment he loses that feeling, he loses any concern for people. He ceases to bear any responsibility for society. On an impulse, he will do things that ordinary people cannot comprehend.

Labour reform does not make a man lose all human feeling. Hunger does.

For whatever reason a man has been sent to do hard labour, he will generally continue to enjoy the sympathy and concern of his family. If a labour reform camp can keep its men supplied with enough food to maintain life, the men will naturally think of and long for their families. It doesn't matter what kind of convict you're talking about.

But the policy of substituting-gourds-and-greens-for-lowered-rations callously broke these family bonds. In fact, relatives on the outside were even less fortunate than the convicts, for they did not know their sons and brothers in the camps had turned into wolves. That they had already turned into automatons that gulped down whatever they could to eat. Family members on the outside had no idea that their relatives on the inside saw them only as chance to get some food, that they had absolutely no love or consideration for them left at all.

I never met a man in the camps at this time who talked about his parents, wife, lover or children in warm, earnest, loving terms – not even the shortest sentence. The exception was that dead convict whose dictionary had failed to tell him he shouldn't eat too much raw corn. That one did show some feelings when he talked about his father.

During rest times, lying on the kang, if we weren't burying our heads and trying to sleep then we were staring with wide blank eyes up at the reed ceiling. I never saw a man bring out a picture of his family. Nobody reminisced, or showed the slightest lingering warmth for relatives. A mention of one's home, that is one's real home, was bound to be related to receiving a package of things to eat in the mail. Home was, pure and simple, a source of supply.

Other than that, home had no place in a man's emotions, because he had lost his emotions. Relatives at home were in a difficult position too. If they were unable to send a man packages, that meant he basically did not even have a home.

Naturally, I was no different. When I wrote my mother letters, they were a sprinkling of words around a long shopping list. If I tried to think of more to write, I would soon return to those things I was in urgent need of. I had been squeezed dry of any tears. In the entries above there are a number of places that say on such and such a day of a month I 'wrote Mama a letter'. The contents of those letters were all the same – they were itemized lists of things I needed.

On the evening of 4 September, though, I suddenly had a nightmare. I became aware of how much, at that very moment, I was tormenting my mother. What led to this discovery of a conscience in myself? What made me suddenly realize that I was not just a machine for eating things, but also some woman's son – to the extent that I could implicitly reprimand myself?

The diary does not record it, because it could not. Escapes, eating greens, making counter-revolutionary statements, stealing, being lazy on the job, playing dead dog – all these things that went against the system were reported by the leaders themselves as they called rollcall. Each one involved a severe 'report', which is to say violent cursing of the offender.

This other sort of matter was not what leaders would report to us in a meeting. Everything that I wrote in this diary was something that the leaders had already told us. In this way, even if the diary fell into the leader's hands, they would have nothing to grab on to when they read it. What the leaders did not report, I did not write down. One can hardly imagine what would have happened later if I had.

Following is a summary of what happened on 4 September 1960. This recounts what I saw myself, and gives the background and additional circumstances from what I heard others say immediately afterwards.

The diary notes that on 4 September we cut green fertilizer on the east side of Canal Nine. Green fertilizer simply meant green grass. If it was used to feed animals after mowing then it was called fodder. For fertilizer, you would bury the mown grass in the ground and let it decompose, then dig it out the second year. The grass was thickest in September, especially along the banks of the canal, where it grew higher than a man.

Over one hundred convicts spread out along the slope of the bank, each carrying his sickle. You may remember from what was written earlier that cutting grass was normally an easy job, bestowed on convicts who were getting lenient treatment. When farm work was busy it was indeed considered a comparatively easy job. Right now, the farm work had let up so all the convicts could take it a little easier. In the luxuriant grass, each person had his own little universe. The Troop Leader would have had a hard time catching them at it anyway, so those who liked toads caught toads, those who fished for small fish went after small fish. Those who habitually stole sunflower seeds stole and ate them.

There were also those who relied on the protection the high grass provided to slip over to the neighbouring sweet-potato fields to dig up a few sweet potatoes. Since only two Troop Leaders were keeping guard over one hundred men, they had to depend on the 'self-awareness' of the convicts themselves. But convicts don't have a high level of self-awareness. As I have written, we were men who were exhausted even before we started out to work. Our small group had been assigned a portion of the canal slope that was right up next to the water. I was Secretary General, so according to custom I and the Leader of our group were assigned to 'hold the sides'. We were to keep the other sixteen convicts between us. This was a measure devised to prevent convicts from escaping; among other things, it expressed a certain trust that the leaders had in their Group Leaders and record keepers. I was also, however, a convict who had become fairly used to escaping. I was one who ate greens, who let down the leaders when they trusted me. In character with these things, taking advantage of the favourable terrain, the first thing I did was burrow through the grass down the canal bank into a sweet-potato field. I used my sickle to dig up several large sweet potatoes.

On return to my appointed place, I cut a lot of grass and put it over these potatoes to hide them. The entry in the diary notes that I 'gave Ding Haiji a sweet potato'. That was where it came from.

You are much more assured of success in your labour reform if you have a few sweet potatoes in hand. In *The Quotations of Chairman Mao*, issued somewhat later, the line I most resonated to was the one that said, 'One can rest assured with grain in hand.'

I had been cutting grass until three or four in the afternoon, when I noticed three people in the distance walking towards us on the top of the canal. One was the postman of the labour reform camp, a man well-known to all the convicts. He often came out to where we were working to pass along orders or instructions to the Troop Leader.

But there was also a young woman leading a four or five-year-old child, and these two we had never seen. When they were almost up to where we were cutting grass, the three of them stopped. The mailman stood at a short distance and waited for the young woman and child to get themselves tidied up. Through the waving grasses, tossed back and forth by the wind, I saw the young woman take a comb out of a black and white bag. The bag had a white design on it against a black background. She bent over to comb the child's hair, then straightened out her little braids. Then she carefully patted the dust off the girl's body and her shoes. I could see it puff out from the child's clothes under the strong sun.

When the young child was properly fixed up, the mother started on herself. I will never forget the way she lifted her two arms to her hair. So elegant, so refined – in that moment she expressed the essence of womanhood. She undid her own braids and combed back her hair, all the while holding a barette in her mouth. As she did this, she turned around and put her back to the mailman, also to the convicts who were working. As though she were playing a piano, her nimble fingers swiftly rose and fell behind her head as she braided her hair. Seen through the tips of the grasses, her tiny waist seemed to be gently swaying.

No woman had ever attracted my attention like this before. Perhaps it was because I had several sweet potatoes hidden in the grass that I felt relaxed enough to enjoy the sight. What happened afterwards froze the scene in my mind for ever. Now, whenever I see a woman raise her arms to comb her hair, not only am I moved by the beauty of this movement, but at the same time I feel a violent premonition that something terrible is going to happen.

Some devil hides behind every kind of beauty.

She had trudged one thousand *li* to get here.* She had come from her home in Gansu Province, from N County in the Hexi Corridor. First she had taken a long-distance bus to Lanzhou, then from Lanzhou she took a train to Y City. From Y to H County, where our labour camp was located, she had travelled entirely on her two legs. There

---

*One *li* equals about one-third of a mile or half a kilometre, but 'a thousand li' is also a figure of speech for any long distance.

is no bus system between Y City and H County, but there is a small road; between the county seat and our camp there is not only no road, there isn't even a regular dirt track. In some better stretches there are sections of village paths. If you want to take a short cut you simply pass through the fields.

She had come over innumerable hills and ditches; she had also passed through a broad muddy stretch of swampy land. Having brought the small child, she must have carried her on her back for some distance, then carried her in front, then let her walk the easier parts on her own. She had walked from early morning until late afternoon, asking who knows how many local villagers the way to the camp. Now, she had finally found the place where her husband was doing labour reform.

The dust on her and on her child recorded the difficulty of their journey. But just before seeing the beloved person for whom she had been longing, she stopped and erased the record of her devotion.

By now, all the convicts cutting grass on the side of the canal had noticed her. The only thing they cared about, however, was the black and white bag she carried. They knew that inside there had to be something to eat. Gulping back saliva as they stared they wondered, 'Whose family is this? Which man will be so lucky today?'

The cloth bag was small – what was packed inside could not amount to much. Still, it had to be enough for one meal. From the size of that pathetic little bag I guessed that she too was having a hard time. She and her daughter would have had to put aside grain from their own 'lowered rations' kernel by kernel for one year to save up what she had brought today.

After a while the three of them walked on, then stopped thirty-some metres away from me on the top of the canal. The woman noticed that the men were all staring at her, so she covered her face and sheltered her child. The child kept peeking her head out to take a curious look at us. I never saw the woman's face clearly, but I could see that she wore a grey so-called 'Lenin uniform', popular among working women at that time. Clearly she was not a farm girl – she was probably a teacher, or a minor cadre like an accountant. Guessing from the child's face and its finely etched eyebrows, the woman's own face had to be handsome.

On the high bank of the canal, the mailman smiled and said a few words to her, then waved out over us with a great sweep of his hand, as though he was trying to explain how our fields were organized.

Then, in a loud voice he shouted down, 'Hey! Where's your Troop Leader?'

We gladly straightened our backs immediately and pretended to search in all directions for the man. The Troop Leader happened to be over on a branch canal haranguing a convict for eating greens.

'There he is! There he is!' In fact, convicts have to be aware at all times of where the Troop Leader is, the way a mouse has to watch out for the cat. Following the directions of our pointing fingers, the postman strode out to talk to him.

Usually a Troop Leader would not allow convicts to see their families in the work-fields. It was against the labour reform system. Since the mailman had walked together from the Main Camp with this woman and her child, though, talking as they walked along, he had begun to feel friendly towards them. So he went to petition the Troop Leader on her behalf. Who knows what he said to the man, but suddenly the Troop Leader erupted in a loud guffaw. Finally he put his head back and barked out the convict's name.

He yelled it several times, and eventually a convict from way over on the big canal slowly stood up. Step by step, he made his way through the thick grass towards the Troop Leader.

I thought to myself, Now we're really going to see something good! This scene is bound to be more moving than any programme in our so-called Evening Entertainment. This will be a veritable 'Meng Jiang looks for her husband'* – but what this modern Meng Jiang will find is not a skeleton but a living, loving husband. It's going to be splendid!

So I too felt fortunate – to be so near the big canal, to be able to steal some sweet potatoes, and to be able to see this bittersweet scene of husband and wife reunited. Wielding my sickle, I pretended to be cutting grass. Half bent over, I cut no more than one stalk at a time, waiting to see the laughter and tears as they embraced one another.

The Troop Leader said a few words to the lucky bastard, who then started to make his way towards our patch on the canal. To this day, I remember the puppet-like way he walked, as though his tall thin body was being manipulated by strings. Like a man with rickets, his head nodded downward at every step. I couldn't help but be upset about this man: his posture, his gait,

---

*This is a story about a wife who goes to look for her husband who has been conscripted to work on building the Great Wall.

everything about him indicated that he and his wife were a badly matched pair.

From a distance, the young woman saw that the Troop Leader had given permission for them to see each other. Leading her child by the hand, she came down the bank of the canal. She could not leap over an invisible barrier and go to meet her husband privately in the security of the deep grass. All she could do was stand at the foot of the canal, waiting for him. Unfortunately, we couldn't see her face – she used her cotton bag to shield it from the sun. Every muscle in her body was focused on watching her husband approach. All I could see of her emotions was that the flimsy cotton bag was trembling.

But when this fortunate husband reached his family, in that most moving instant, he did not hug the child or give any indication of feelings for his wife. I was standing closer to them than anyone else, and I could just make out her trembling voice as she started speaking to him. Without letting her finish, he snatched the cotton bag from her like a robber. As fast as he could, he crawled up the bank of the canal to the top.

There was a small willow tree up there, which afforded at least a little bit of shade. He didn't even take time to select a place to sit. He threw himself down, in the full sun, and urgently ripped at the fabric. His two elbows were cocked outwards, like a man pulling a bow, while his ten fingers violently pulled the bag apart. Then he began stuffing the things inside into his mouth.

The scene that I had hoped would move me, would restore my humanity a little, amounted to nothing more than these ten short seconds!

Disappointed, I bent down and began to cut grass in earnest. I was unwilling to torment myself any further.

Staring at someone eating when you are not is worse than watching a bully humiliate your wife when you have no ability to defend her. Zhu Zhenbang was assigned to work beside me on this day, however, and he stood there watching everything that happened on top of the canal. A criminal convict, he had no compunction about openly stopping his work.

'Damn,' he said after a while. 'The dogshitter's eating flatbread!'

After a few more moments he reported, 'Ah! Motherfucker! She brought eggs for him!' From time to time he would mutter to himself, 'Eh? What's that he's eating? Can't make it out,' until his mouth was swimming in saliva, and so was mine.

Although I forbade myself to look, from time to time I couldn't help just glancing up at the canal. I should say here that this young woman was a revelation to me. From then on, she epitomized a good wife. One who took care of her husband, who showed consideration, who was the image of and the specific embodiment of a good mate. She did not follow her husband up to the top of the canal but stayed sitting at the bottom, her child cradled in her arms. Her face was turned slightly to one side: she was silently crying. Her daughter, with her little fist in her mouth, was eagerly looking up at her father. From the intentness with which she watched him eat, it was clear that she too was famished. At the very least, she had had nothing to eat all day. If the mother took her up to join her father, naturally she would want to eat some of his food. The way the child was cradled implied that she was being held back.

And so, just like me when I traded my pants for watermelons, he ate easy up there on the bank. Oblivious of the searing sun above and the whole world below, he just put his head down and ate. The shade was a few feet away but he didn't even roll over to take advantage of it. Sweat poured down his face. As he started eating, I heard him cough when the food got caught in his throat; after that, it went down more easily. She sat below, quietly crying. He sat above, quietly eating.

Zhu Zhenbang decided that there was nothing more to see or hear. Disgusted, he gave a long, deep sigh, then sullenly bent down to cut the grass before him.

After around forty minutes, I had almost forgotten them. I was immersed in the problem of how to get my stolen sweet potatoes home to the barracks without being caught. If I made a mistake, not only would my labours be wasted but I would have to be photographed. Photographing was not so bad now, but it would be a real shame to have the sweet potatoes confiscated. I still had not thought up a workable plan when I heard a piercing, gut-rending cry from above.

Many terrible things happened in the labour reform camps, but I had never experienced a scream that set my whole body to shaking. Goosebumps violently erupted all over me. The cry came from the top of the canal. By the time we looked up, all we saw was the little girl standing there sobbing.

The young woman was nowhere to be seen. Nor was the convict.

We could not transgress the invisible line of authority and run over to see what had happened, of course, so we turned our heads in the other direction and searched for the Troop Leader. He had also heard the scream in the distance, and he came rushing towards the canal bank in great flying steps. In no time at all he was on top. We saw him stiffen as he looked down into the flowing water.

The Troop Leader was the kind of man who is unashamed of being Troop Leader. He froze for no more than a second, then whipped around and called the other Troop Leader. The other Troop Leader arrived in record time. The two had a few words together on top of the canal, then they called down to me to find four particular criminal convicts whose bodies had not yet broken down. They also wanted four female convicts. They gave me the names.

I forgot to think about breathing, and I didn't even cough. Excited, I raised my two arms and passed along the Troop Leader's order. It was passed on to the convicts in the furthest corners of the grass. Eight men and women soon appeared, none of whom I knew. Somehow, who knows where the ability comes from, I could remember their names perfectly after the Troop Leader had said them just once.

The eight men and women convicts climbed up the bank. As they looked over at the water rushing on the other side, I could hear their long, chilling sighs. I even heard one of the female convicts say, 'Mother, oh Mother.'

Among these women was the actress who had stuck her tongue out at me. I had no idea which name belonged to whom, however. At that moment, as though they were getting ready to do battle with a huge enemy, the two Troop Leaders cracked the ropes that had been tied at their waists. Brandishing them, they advanced viciously on the eight convicts.

'What are you looking at? Move! Get going!'

One Troop Leader supervised. He ordered the eight

convicts to take an arm and leg each and lift up the man and wife. The other Troop Leader snapped his rope at us convicts working below, at the same time blocking our line of sight.

'Get to work. Harder! You're going to finish that job today if it kills you. Back to work.'

The Troop Leader then called out the names of several Group Leaders that he most trusted. 'All right, listen here. Those who haven't put enough work in today will be dealt with when we get back. We'll settle up accounts.'

'Settling accounts' was a terrible thing to hear. No matter what method was used to do the accounting, the convict always did the paying. A light punishment would mean something physical; heavier punishment meant the date of your graduation was affected. The convicts were supremely curious about what had happened, but there was nothing they could do but bend over and begin to cut grass hard. Soon the entire area was swishing with the sound of their sickles, and the piercing scream of the woman was only an echo in my mind.

The eight convicts first spread the man and woman out on the muddy ground on top of the embankment. Then, under the direction of the Troop Leader, the men lifted the man and the women lifted the woman. Chanting a work song to keep in step, they swayed forward to the Main Camp.

One Troop Leader followed behind them. With twice the responsibility on his shoulders, Troop Leader Zheng now had to be twice as fierce. He flew back and forth along the bank where we were working, striking out at almost every convict he saw. The rope in his hand danced wildly to and fro. Many convicts suffered that day. Going home after work, many hands and faces carried the wounds. In the diary, this was recorded as 'Troop Leader Zheng got angry.'

Since our small group was closest to the side of the large canal, not on the periphery, he actually beat us less. We were spared the rope, but since we had cut less grass at the end of the day our group was punished by being made to 'work an additional hour'.

What is written above explains what was put in the diary. Below I should explain what did not get written into the diary.

What had that lucky convict done to make his wife let out such a heart-rending scream? Wasn't he sitting there eating easy, gnawing away on the flatbread and eggs his wife had brought?

He was. But when he had finished, he took the sickle with which he had been cutting grass and swiftly slit the veins on his wrists. From the force of this action, he fell down towards the inside of the bank of the canal.

One slice of a knife doesn't take any longer than the blink of an eye. Wiping her teary eyes, his wife had not seen it happen. After a while, when she turned around and saw only the empty black and white bag like a dead seagull on the ground, she simply thought her husband had gone to relieve himself. After eating so much, having to relieve himself was quite natural.

After another stretch of time, she led the child on up the bank. All the food's been eaten, she was probably thinking, and he's good and full – now would be a good time to sit and talk. At the top of the canal she found her husband upside down – head facing downward on the canal slope. Fresh red blood was flowing from his veins into the water from the Yellow River, dyeing the muddy brown a dark dark red. From the amount of blood, the river seemed to have started red at its source.

She let out the scream that I cannot forget, and then collapsed beside her husband's body.

As I write, I try to figure out the rationale behind it, but I still cannot understand why her husband committed suicide. Why he should do it at precisely that moment, and why he had to do it right there in front of his wife and child? The fact of suicide itself is understandable, but he could have waited until after they left and still have had time to do it, or he could have accomplished it before they arrived.

Those who had never done labour reform say that he was dying of hunger. He didn't even think of his wife and child until after he had eaten his full – then he suddenly discovered that they too were starving, so he committed suicide out of shame. This theory is without merit. When relatives came to see convicts in the camps, they were given the right to a guest-pass for food. In the diary I recorded an instance of falsely declaring that I had a visitor – I tried to get an extra ration but was unsuccessful and got cursed by the leaders. Also, after Ma Weixiao's family came to see him I asked him to get a guest ration for me.

There is no doubt that his wife and child were also starving, but he could instantly have produced two rations of food for them to eat. He was the kind of convict who makes a pretty good representation of himself – every time we had the Thought Line-up, or an Evaluation of Advanced Behaviour, he was always among the first few names. Generally speaking, the labour reform camp gave lenient treatment to this kind of convict;

sometimes it would even let couples spend a night together.

Some people felt that he wanted to punish his wife, that he committed suicide in front of her on purpose. These too were people with no understanding of the situation. According to convicts who knew him, not only had his wife refrained from proposing that they be divorced, on his account she had been sent from the city to the countryside to teach in a small village school. It is hard to believe he would punish such a virtuous wife, who had also travelled a thousand li to see him.

Still others said he was thinking of the future of his wife and child. Only after he was dead could she thoroughly dissociate herself from him, draw a line between them, so that one day her situation might be a little better. Even so, one returns to that original question: couldn't he have waited until the two of them had left?

There was a great deal of debate after this event. I was inclined to only one explanation. A convict from his group said this man had once told him in the past: 'I'd rather be a ghost who died from over-stuffing than a ghost who died from hunger! The Buddhist classics speak of six ways one can be reincarnated. There is hell, hungry ghosts, animals, Asura, humans and heaven, and the worst of these is to become a hungry ghost.'

He had been a member of the Communist Youth League, and then he taught political science in the middle school of N County. He and his wife had graduated together from a teachers' college; together they were assigned to teach in the same school. In peer reviews the two of them had been classified as 'front-line, advanced workers'. But the political-science textbooks in middle school include some philosophy. From these books, he became infatuated with that most difficult of academic disciplines, Buddhism. One day, as a text was being recited in class, he suddenly announced what was really in his mind. As though obsessed, he declared, 'There is no clear distinction between idealism and materialism.' He went on the describe reasons that he personally thought were valid to explain this heretical statement.

In fact, whether or not idealism and materialism have any precise distinction, just where the line is and so on, is something that can be discussed calmly at any academic conference. But intellectuals had not been trained to discuss academic questions; they were trained to regard all academic issues as political questions. As a result, all the intellectuals, both great and small, in N County published their opinions on the subject.

'What are you trying to say – is there no clear distinction between peasants and landlords?'

'So there is no distinction between workers and capitalists, is there!'

'Is it going too far to say that you are blurring the line between Communist theory and rotten capitalism?'

'I ask you, during the war to defend Korea against the Americans, was there no precise line between invaders and defenders?'

'You mean there is no line between the socialist camp and the imperialist camp?'

On a path paved with innumerable question marks, he slid suddenly down to the bottom of a pit. The result, quite understandably, was that he was hatted with the accusation of 'rightist'.

Under the 'thought guidance' of 'correctly-dealing-with-internal-contradictions-among-the-people' he was dealt with lightly. He wasn't judged an enemy-of-the-people. He was merely sent off to do hard labour.

N County was a backward little place; he was a graduate of a very average teachers' college. In such a place, he had depended on his own diligent self-study and had burrowed as far as he could into fundamental questions that many philosophers have never figured out. It was clear that he was a thinking man, and that he was a man of a strongly rational nature. Only this kind of man would find it amusing to argue over details, as we say to 'drill into the very tip of a cow-horn'. As has been mentioned, he represented himself well in the camps. He was very proper and he never exhibited irrational behaviour. So why should he, only now, only here, suddenly use a sickle to cut open his veins?

He had not lost his reason but rather his emotions. He no longer had the slightest interest in his wife or child. He cared nothing about the human race, or the entire world, or the issues about which he had formerly cared so strongly. He had even ceased to be interested in eating – if he had ever wanted to eat again, he would not have committed suicide.

I now knew what the renegade Zhu Zhenbang meant when he talked about using a wooden knife to kill a man. Such a knife was aimed not at a man's throat, chest or stomach. Instead it attacked the invisible feelings that tied him to the world around him. A wooden knife could not enter a man's flesh, but it was plenty sharp enough to cut immaterial things.

Before leaving for the barracks after work that day, more than one hundred convicts had to line up beside the canal for rollcall. They could not return home until their names had been checked against the list. The convicts took the opportunity of being near the scene of the action to rush together to the top of the bank. Troop Leader Zheng was only one man with one rope – there was no way he could stop them. He lashed out wildly anyway, screaming curses all the while. Only with the greatest difficulty did he finally get this unruly herd of animals to come down from the canal. His anger had to find a mark, and it found its aim in our small group.

'Just look at you. Eighteen of you animals and you've managed to cut such a pitiful amount of grass. There's no point in complaining about you. It doesn't work. Heh Cheng!' Our Group Leader, the rather well qualified engineer, immediately stood straight, perked up his ears and looked at the Troop Leader with the eyes of a dog looking up at its master. 'You listen to me. You'll cut tonight until you can't see the grass. You're not allowed to come back until then.'

He herded the other one hundred convicts back to their barracks, until only eighteen men were left in the work-field. I was truly fortunate that day! The shield of night-time was boundless – by the time we went home I could practically carry my sweet potatoes out in the open. Swinging along happily behind the line of men, I held them to my bosom in my tattered shirt. Obviously, it is pointless to waste time in trying to control things – not even the most marvellous, carefully thought-out plans can surpass the serendipity of chance.

The curtain of evening had fallen by the time I crawled up the bank of the canal to have a look. I could only smell the odour – the fleeting fragrance, faint and sweet, of raw blood. It smelled as though it was being wafted from a distant place, but then again as though it came from right under my nose. The water was still flowing, with a delicate murmur, but it didn't say anything to me that was counter-revolutionary.

The small black and white bag had disappeared. The eighteen of us looked for it for quite some time but didn't find it. I had clearly seen it lying there on the bank of the canal after those eight male and female convicts carried the two of them away. Maybe one of the convicts snatched it up just before quitting work.

Psychologists think that a particular stimulus on a young mind may influence a child for a lifetime. It makes one wonder about that young child with the braids, that little girl with the clear, intelligent eyes. Sucking on her fist, she had looked up towards her father, wishing that Daddy might give her something to eat, or might even give her a little warmth, some fatherly love. In the end what she saw was Daddy's fresh blood flowing like a river.

I wonder where she is now. How she survived those hard times.

Has the colour of the blood faded in your mind? If you are alive, you should be around thirty today. If you ever read this book, I would like to let you know:

> I am willing to do everything for you,
> Just so long as you can be happy.